PRIMERS

Practical Poetics in Architecture

WILEY

PRIMERS

Practical Poetics in Architecture

LEON VAN SCHAIK

WILEY

©2015 John Wiley & Sons Ltd

Registered office
John Wiley & Sons Ltd, The Atrium, Southern Gate, Chichester, West Sussex, PO19 8SQ,
United Kingdom

For details of our global editorial offices, for customer services and for information about
how to apply for permission to reuse the copyright material in this book please see our
website at www.wiley.com.

The right of the author to be identified as the author of this work has been asserted in
accordance with the Copyright, Designs and Patents Act 1988.

Wiley publishes in a variety of print and electronic formats and by print-on-demand. Some
material included with standard print versions of this book may not be included in e-books or
in print-on-demand. If this book refers to media such as a CD or DVD that is not included in
the version you purchased, you may download this material at http://booksupport.wiley.com.
For more information about Wiley products, visit www.wiley.com.

Designations used by companies to distinguish their products are often claimed as
trademarks. All brand names and product names used in this book are trade names, service
marks, trademarks or registered trademarks of their respective owners. The publisher is not
associated with any product or vendor mentioned in this book. This publication is designed
to provide accurate and authoritative information in regard to the subject matter covered.
It is sold on the understanding that the publisher is not engaged in rendering professional
services. If professional advice or other expert assistance is required, the services of a
competent professional should be sought.

Executive Commissioning Editor: Helen Castle
Production Editor: David Sassian
Assistant Editor: Calver Lezama

ISBN 978-1-118-82889-2 (paperback)
ISBN 978-1-118-82892-2 (ebk)
ISBN 978-1-118-82894-6 (ebk)
ISBN 978-1-118-82893-9 (ebk)
ISBN 978-1-118-82888-5 (ebk)

Cover design, page design and layouts by Karen Willcox, www.karenwillcox.com
Cover image ©Peter Bennetts
Printed in Italy by Printer Trento Srl

I dedicate this book to all those who strive in the immensely complex practice of architecture.

Acknowledgements

I acknowledge with great gratitude the help of my assistant Melisa McDonald, and of the publishing team: Helen Castle, the commissioning editor at Wiley; Calver Lezama, her assistant; Abigail Grater, the copy editor; and Karen Willcox, the designer. I am also indebted to successive editors of *Architecture Australia* and *Architectural Review* who have given me the opportunity to develop a style of reviewing, in particular Cameron Bruhn and Michael Holt. The architects who feature are central to the book, and their candour is the lifeline of my research. I am especially indebted to Esther Anatolitis, Vivian Mitsogianni, Ayse Senturer and Zeynep Mennan, as well as to Andrew Keen and Michael Spooner for their comments on the introductory essay and on sample case studies. I hope they find that the book merits a second reading. In the back of my mind, I have imagined the book being read by mentors and friends like William and Lena Lim, Peter Cook and Yael Reisner, CJ Lim, Will Hunter, Catherine Stutterheim, and all the architects and architects in the making I have ever had the pleasure to work with thus far.

Contents

Preface

Conversations and their inherent feedback loops construct knowledge. They bring together the observations and understandings of different people in the pursuit of common projects.[1] During 2013 I had several conversations with Helen Castle, Executive Commissioning Editor on the global Architecture list at Wiley, and Kate Goodwin, Drue Heinz Curator of Architecture at the Royal Academy of Arts (RA). These arose because Kate, who was working on the exhibition 'Sensing Spaces: Architecture Reimagined' at the RA in London (25 January – 6 April 2014) was reading my essay on poetics and my book on spatial intelligence and had sought an introduction to me through Helen, the publisher.[2] Kate and I discussed the use of conversation as a curatorial tool, much as I have discovered it to be a tool used in various ways of designing.

This led to Helen wondering whether there was a book that could capture more recent knowledge about poetics in architectural practice, my field of research. 'So much is written about poetics in architecture, but so little is demonstrated' was my response. Developing the idea for the book, my driving idea was: 'We don't need more theory, we need to show how poetics supports the design practice of architects!'

Kate completed her exhibition working with featured architects and practices: Grafton Architects, Diébédo Francis Kéré, Kengo Kuma, Li Xiaodong, Pezo von Ellrichshausen, Álvaro Siza and Eduardo Souto de Moura. She created for the very first time in a major gallery an installation that aimed at getting a

Peter Lyssiotis, Montage, Melbourne, 1998
While this image may be read as surrealist, prosaically it evokes an insight into what could be done to a door to enable a view of a crescent moon.

public to appreciate and engage with poetic and sensory aspects of architecture through their own experience of the show. The hope was that the public (largely non-architects) would use and/or build on their own spatial intelligence in the process of engaging with the exhibits. A debate was sparked among architects as well, much of it concerning the fine line between architecture as a practice and as an autonomous activity – which, outside the 15-year-old project of London's Serpentine Gallery pavilions, it seldom is. The exhibition, illustrated here with three images, certainly achieved its goal, and was a popular success.

'Sensing Spaces: Architecture Reimagined', Royal Academy of Arts, London, 25 January to 6 April 2014 (curated by Kate Goodwin): installation by Grafton Architects
This installation completely reversed the spatial configuration of the gallery, although conforming to the same top-lit paradigm. The space shifts from being one that rises to rooflights that wash the walls, to a weighty space with paradoxically elusive connections to the ground.

For this book, more directly aimed at practitioners and students, but also at those wishing to deepen their understanding of architecture, I have assembled 22 case studies, selecting a range of projects by architects whose work I have been following for several years. I met the architects at the sites of the selected projects, and uncovered through conversation the moment that a poetic threshold was crossed and their design ideas flowed. My task was not easy. Consciousness itself is the subject, and while all humans have this, no one knows what it is. So revealing how it works in designing is rather like trying to catch a butterfly in a net while looking sideways. And inescapably the net is a poor tool, being composed of current knowledge and the known gaps in that knowledge – nets are holes held in a web of experience. Nonetheless I believed that these architects could provide solid evidence of the role of poetics in designing.

As I talked to the architects, we were grappling with the origins of architectural ideas, delving into the mental space that architects construct in order to design, trying to isolate the mental frames that they marshal and bring into play on the field of their designing.[3] This involved trying to get mental fingers onto the edges of their consciousness as they designed, acting as a detective, finding clues by exploring their designing mind-sets

'Sensing Spaces: Architecture Reimagined', Royal Academy of Arts, London, 25 January to 6 April 2014 (curated by Kate Goodwin): installation by Pezo von Ellrichshausen
An installation that brought people into contact with the details of the gallery. Designed to be seen from far below, this intimate relationship to the detail was startling, as was the appreciation of the actual rather than the apparent height of the space.

'Sensing Spaces: Architecture Reimagined', Royal Academy of Arts, London, 25 January to 6 April 2014 (curated by Kate Goodwin): installation by Li Xiaodong
A wintry external space was created within the warm Beaux-Arts interior of the gallery. Offsetting this behind one of these grey sapling walls was a glowing honey-coloured cabin interior.

after the completion of their projects. Because nothing exists until it is observed,[4] and the act of observing is – as I argued in my diploma thesis in 1968 – necessarily a framing act: 'The Consultant Arrives and Sees' what he or she has been trained to see, has learned to see, comes to see through each new conversation.[5] Concepts in my essay on poetics and in the book on spatial intelligence were strong mental frames for me, as were many years of conversations with these and scores of other architects about their ways of designing.[6]

It was a vital part of the research for this book that these frames were exposed to the architects. For this book the conversation centred on a specific project. This was documented in field notes, then framed in an ideogram that located the anecdotes – those crucial nuggets of architectural knowledge – in their various theoretical homes. A written account of the conversation followed and it was sent with its ideogram to the architects for them to check for factual and conceptual accuracy.[7] This is unusual practice, but here there is a deliberate extension of the feedback conventions of conversations, so that I could say to the architects: 'Here is what I have learned, and this is how I have framed it in my mental net. Have I been true to our conversations? Is this a good account of what happened in the project? Is it accurate enough for others to learn from it?'

After this, without reference to anyone else, I selected a 'companion' project to sit alongside each case study, a project that seems to me to have similar poetics. I want to show the broader extent of these poetic ambitions.

What has resulted is a book consisting of a broad introduction to the use of the concept of poetics in architecture and 22 case studies. These identify poetic thresholds in projects, those moments when a platform of insight is established and designing begins to flow. This, I argue, is when poetics is practical, when it provides the trigger for design action.

References

1. See Gordon Pask, *Conversation, Cognition and Learning: A Cybernetic Theory and Methodology*, Elsevier (Amsterdam, Oxford and London), 1975.
2. Leon van Schaik, *Poetics in Architecture*, Wiley (Chichester), 2002, pp 5–11 and 95–7; Leon van Schaik, *Spatial Intelligence: New Futures for Architecture*, Wiley (Chichester), 2008.
3. See Mark Turner, *The Origin of Ideas: Blending, Creativity, and the Human Spark*, Oxford University Press (Oxford), 2014.
4. See Robert Lanza and Bob Berman, *Biocentrism: How Life and Consciousness are the Keys to Understanding the True Nature of the Universe*, Ben Bella Books (Dallas, TX), 2009.
5. Leon van Schaik, *Descent into the Street*, diploma thesis, Architectural Association, London, 1968. 'The Consultant Arrives and Sees' is the caption to an ideogram in the thesis.
6. See Leon van Schaik, *Mastering Architecture: Becoming a Creative Innovator in Practice*, Wiley (Chichester), 2005.
7. With one exception – as indicated in the notes to that case study, the University of Cincinnati case study was based on earlier research.

Introduction

Architecture is a practice that arises from spatial thinking. It addresses the world and our presence in it spatially, organising material in pursuit of physical and virtual ideas. Like everything in our material culture, every act of architecture has its poetics, that is to say a 'reading' specific to its conception and realisation. To understand this poetics is to understand individual and communal histories in space and the values these have imbued in each architect. It is also to understand the political position of every act of architecture because, unlike more autonomous arts, architecture acts upon those who build it and on those who occupy it. Practical poetics, like practical criticism,[1] is an approach to the poetic in architecture that seeks to separate authentic architectural poetics from clichéd and sentimental design tropes that evoke immediate and shallow stock responses in observers and users. Without this understanding architecture struggles to register its power to help society in its pursuit of wellbeing, and is relegated to being a symbolic backdrop to transitory acts of consumption.

What is poetics? Strictly speaking, poetics is the theory of literature and it concerns how poetry and other creative writing should be 'read' – that is, understood and evaluated. It therefore has an impact on how writers – who are often also critics – write. In architecture, poetics has come to fill a similar role. Architects, of the kind included in this book and their like, when they are advanced in their research into programme, site, materials and construction possibilities, 'read' the situation of a project as a whole. Thus they establish

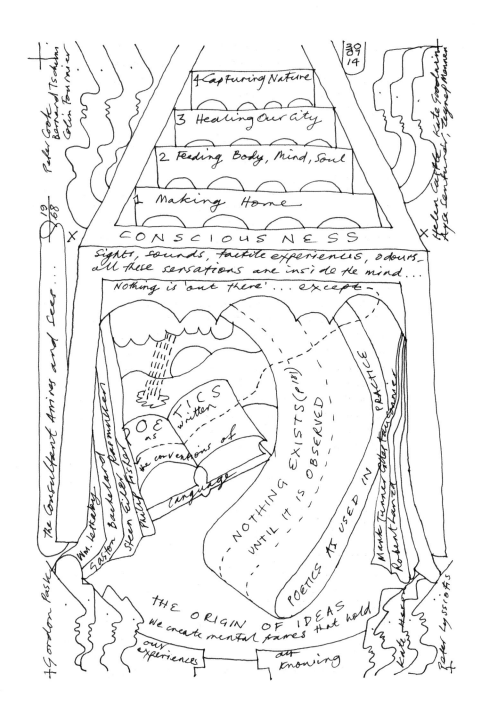

4 Capturing Nature

3 Healing Our City

2 Feeding Body, Mind, Soul

1 Making Home

C O N S C I O U S N E S S

Sights, sounds, tactile experiences, odours, all these sensations are inside the mind...

Nothing is 'out there'... except—

POETICS as written

the conventions of language

NOTHING EXISTS (p.108) UNTIL IT IS OBSERVED

POETICS AS USED IN PRACTICE

THE ORIGIN OF IDEAS
We create mental frames that hold our experiences / all knowing

Peter Cook, Bernard Tschumi, Colin Fournier

19/68

The Consultant Arrives and Sees ....

Wm. Letaby, Gaston Bachelard, Sven Gösta Permutter, Philip Pistol

+Gordon Pask

Helen Castle, Kate Goodwin, Kya Central, Zygof Manna

Mark Turner, Gilles Fauconnier, Robert Lanza

Kate Heron

Peter Lyssiotis

a poetics that becomes a pathway to a resolved design. When so conceived, this design in turn embodies a poetics in that it is 'readable'. This readability enables the architects to invite clients, users and critics to enter into the mental space that informed the design. Feedback loops of understanding, evaluating and critiquing thus enhance the design practice.

Poetics came into use in architecture when Gaston Bachelard's 1957 book *The Poetics of Space* was published.[2] He made a connection between writing and architecture because he lacked any language other than existing poetry to capture his spatial experience in its full cultural richness. For many decades his leap of faith has inspired students and architects, giving them the courage to use complex cultural information when designing. Bachelard's poetics was embraced in a reaction to the hard materialist thinking of modern architecture that prevailed when he wrote. As such the book served as a benign corrective; but there has been a catch. Too often descriptions in the book are used as briefs for the designing of spaces. This is a burden that they cannot carry. Naïve adopters expect that designs made to fit Bachelard's exquisite accounts of 'roundness' in his chapter on 'Nests' or of the qualities of interiority in his chapter on 'Drawers, Chests and Wardrobes' expect to embrace users in the sentiments of the poetry quoted by Bachelard and held in mind by the designer.[3] This is an illusory belief. Only the designer has the poetry in mind, as is proved by Giuseppe Terragni's unbuilt *Danteum* (designed 1942), that most ambitious attempt to evoke a poem through an architectural design.[4] Although designed with meticulous reference to Dante's poem, understanding this relationship requires the use of an elaborate manual. The architectural reality of the design insists on its own autonomous presence, no matter how hard each space is labelled. A more nuanced understanding of how poetics may act positively in design is needed.

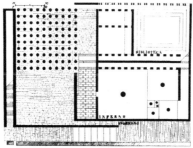

Giuseppe Terragni, *The Danteum*, 1938
The plan is intended to represent the canticles of Dante's *Divine Comedy*.

FIG. 18. Danteum plan at 1.60m.

It is also evident that Bachelard's choice of poems and instances is specific to a region of France. This makes some of his assumptions seem of the province rather than of the world: his definition of the house as being a 'vertical being', for example.[5] However, Bachelard does not succumb to the mystical and (I believe)

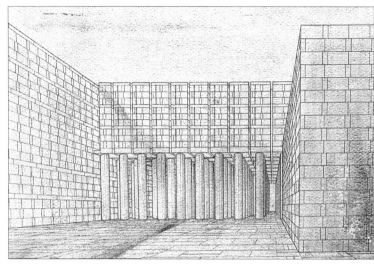

FIG. 108. Danteum, detail of courtyard.

The Danteum, Giuseppe Terragni 1938
View of a courtyard leading to a columnar hall that is intended to evoke a forest.

atavistic, tribal special-pleading for essences of place that plague those influenced by the phenomenological philosophy of Martin Heidegger: Christian Norberg-Schulz and Juhani Pallasmaa among them.[6] So rooted is his thinking in the actualities of specific spaces, following Bachelard does not lead to an art-for-art's-sake approach to designing.

Yet the sentiments Bachelard captures, recognisable as they are even as our own experience disputes their detail, are not directly generalisable. Architects need to establish their own understandings of the roots and origins of the poetics they create. The differentiation process that reinforces regional histories and cultures as ever-growing global corporatisation diminishes the centrifugal power of nation-states risks cementing cultures into caricatures of themselves. Unless creative elites, including architects, articulate the ways in which their mental space frames the poetics that their work embodies, borders are intensified, as are the dangers of self-parody. This leads to architecture that evokes stock responses rather than engagement.

Theorists other than Bachelard, but with a similar passion for the specific poetics of architecture and a distaste for ineffable mystique, provide clues on how to manifest a readable poetics in a work of architecture. A new conception of poetics in Architecture stands head and shoulders on their thinking, and their work repays close study. However, as I will describe, the main thrust of this book is to argue that the way to understanding lies through detailed examination of how architects establish the poetic insights from which their designing cascades.

The Concept of an Architectural Reality as the Basis for the Practical Use of Poetics in Architecture

A chain of theorists have worked to understand how architecture achieves a readable poetics. The architect and critic William Lethaby (1857–1931), who pioneered the use of concrete in church construction and redesigned Melsetter House on the Island of Orkney in Arts and Crafts mode in the late 1890s,[7] argued that architecture as opposed to building always embodies the understanding of the universe current at the time of its making. A lover of pre-Second World War London and Venice, the Danish critic Steen Eiler Rasmussen (1898–1990) used his experience of specific cities and buildings to isolate a series of architectonic qualities (solids and cavities, colour planes, scale and proportion, rhythm, texture, light and sound among them) that will occur in any work of architecture that has readable poetics.[8] The inspirational educator and lover of cities Colin Rowe (1920–1999) set out to prove that city form embodies poetics that are specific to their histories, and that the form itself has practical impacts on the kinds of lives that can be lived in city neighbourhoods.[9] He argued (in my terms) that great cities

Stonehenge, Wiltshire, England, c 3000 BC
A capped ring of large stones known as sarsens, 9 metres (30 feet) tall and weighing 25 tons. Seen here at a summer sunrise.

contain competing districts dedicated to different poetics. Kenneth Frampton, a champion of tectonics and rigour, has fought for legibility and clarity of intention in designing that eschews the elision of concepts in the belief that, despite regional differences, there is a universalisable poetics in architectural endeavour.[10] Dalibor Vesely, the Czech-born Cambridge educator, has championed cities layered with architecture in palimpsests that record the differing ambitions of generations.[11] He has led generations of students to appreciate the full palette of architectural textures that can be used in designing for specific poetics. Like the author, who studies the ways in which architects develop their spatial thinking,[12] all postulate in their own ways an architectural reality distinct from other realities, one that has its own laws and what is termed – in opposition to natural or everyday language – its own 'formal' language. Its own poetics.

Ontologies and Poetics

Reading is not an abstract intellectual activity.[13] It takes place in contexts, and the readability of any given poetics depends on a not always self-evident idea about the history of architecture and of its implied origins as a human activity. Every work of architecture stakes a position about the origins of architecture and about its proper future. Throughout history, Lethaby argued, architects have sought to capture their society's understanding of the universe by marking natural phenomena, creating measuring tools for these, housing and articulating epics and myths, sanctifying the domestic, delineating the sacred, giving form to the processions of religious rituals inside (communal) and outside (hierarchical).[14] Architecture reified the magic through which shamans attempted to control the impact of events on their communities. Psychologists argue that the pursuit of reification began with an architecture that dealt with the drive to survive, before evolving through stages into a tool of power, of order, and of linear and then systems reasoning.[15] At its outset, architecture caught the moment of the solstice, a time of year that signalled the waxing of the sun, so crucial to survival.

The many and varied taxonomic orderings of libraries express the emergence of the architecture of reason,[16] and this finds its expression, for example, in the glories of Sir Christopher Wren's library at Trinity College, Cambridge (1695). Then Architecture assisted in the recursive processes of modernity – observing, theorising, testing and presenting – by housing

Illustration of the Royal Institution, Albemarle Street, from Augustus Pugin and Thomas Rowlandson's *The Microcosm of London or London in Miniature*, 1808–10
Pugin and Rowlandson documented the interiors that housed the emerging institutions of London, from this library meeting room to the coffee house in which among other things banking syndicates were formed.

ROYAL INSTITUTION
ALBEMARLE STREET.

the emerging institutions of modernity in the great rooms of the first 'world city': London.[17] Now, in the Anthropocene (the age in which what changes the surface of the planet is its occupation by humans), Architecture is preoccupied with sustaining life. The pavilion by architects MVRDV at Expo 2000 in Hanover, Germany, opened the 21st century with an iconic manifesto for this position.

As architecture evolved through these stages, it has been argued to embody at each stage three distinct and sometimes conflicting tectonic orders, each with a determining influence on any poetics forged in its context. These orders are master-building, weaving and ideation.

Architect as Master Builder

The theorists and historians Kenneth Frampton and Joseph Rykwert see Architecture as a master-builder tradition with a tectonic ethos arising from the transition from timber shelters to masonry construction.[18] The politics of this celebration of 'the primitive hut' ties architecture to the innocence of the 'noble savage' of Jean-Jacques Rousseau (1712–1778) and to the same

Charles-Dominique-Joseph Eisen, frontispiece to Marc-Antoine Laugier's *An Essay on Architecture*, 1753
The image depicts a muse reclining on the masonry elements that evolved from the archetypal timber hut.

MVRDV, Netherlands Pavilion at Expo 2000, Hanover, Germany, 2000
This pavilion stacked six Dutch landscapes one on top of the other.

philosopher's statement that 'man is born free and everywhere is in chains'.[19]

This modernising ideology embeds the notion of continuous progress and it argues that if architects reject the chains of habit and respect its 'true' origins, then architecture has the power to set society free.[20] In this lineage, a memory of post-and-lintel timber construction well grounded on rock footings is retained in the orders of classical architecture. This logic is re-presented – as in the early architecture of Aldo Rossi (1931–1997)[21] – stripped of the decorations and emphasising its underlying geometry.

Overtly it aims to speak an international language of austere stoicism in the face of changing circumstances. In reaction to the architecture of the spectacle spread by globalisation, there is an appeal to the fundamental commonality in human aspirations and the promise of an escape from the floods of ephemeral imagery that swamp the internet in value-free overabundance. This is a poetics that frames the efforts of many architects discussed in this book (companion architects in parentheses): Joost Bakker (CJ Lim), Jo Van Den Berghe (Clancy Moore), Kurtogpi Architects (McGarry Ní Éanaigh Architects), Sean Godsell Architects (Lina Bo Bardi) and Kerstin Thompson Architects (John Wardle Architects).

Architect as Weaver

Gottfried Semper (1803–1879), a neoclassicist himself, argued that crucial elements of Architecture arose from tent making and the weaving – usually by women – that makes that possible,[22] and this ontology posits an inclusive future for architecture that responds to the regular advances in the technology inherent in the process of weaving. This promotion of a tie to an always evolving technology contrasts with classicism's and modernism's longing for an ancient tectonic ideal. The architect-as-weaver lineage embraces the present and any technology that addresses contemporary

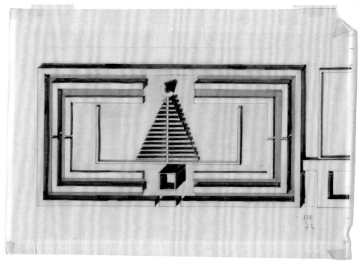

Aldo Rossi, plan for San Cataldo Cemetery at Modena, Italy, 1971
Rossi believed that architecture composed only of the elements of Platonic geometry – cylinder, cone, cube and sphere – would talk to everyone.

concerns, parametric designing – a kind of weaving – included. How did Semper, an accomplished classicist, make this intellectual leap? Ironically it was because he was so rigorous in his classicism that he emphasised the post-and-lintel ideal of timber construction and regarded the walls as separate fabric, preferably woven tapestries. There is a Gothic urge hidden in Semper's reasoning: his view parallels Gothic architecture's extreme disaggregation of structure and wall, epitomised in Paris's Sainte-Chapelle (1248), and its

Carpeted interior of a nomadic tent
In his 1860 treatise *Der Stil in der technischen und tektonischen Künsten* (Style in the Technical and Tectonic Arts), Gottfried Semper articulated a 'theory of clothing' as the origin of architecture, referring to the richly carpeted interiors of the tents of nomads.

Sainte-Chapelle, Paris, 1248
Perhaps the most extreme dissolving away of the wall achieved in Gothic architecture.

testing to destruction of structural ideas, as in the extreme height that led to the collapse in 1284 of the nave of the cathedral in the French town of Beauvais. Both of these adventures, success and failure, are a far cry from the conservatism innate in the classical 'primitive hut' ontology.

The pragmatic adventurousness of Gothic architecture has an extraordinarily flexible manifestation in humbler institutional buildings and in domestic architecture. Where classical axiality bounded figures in the nine-square ideal,[23] the bay-by-bay extendability of medieval architecture as seen in structures such as Little Moreton Hall in Cheshire (1504–1610) prefigures the more organic architectures that parametrics allow.

Carpentry, masonry and parametrics depend for their raw materials and advancement on elites of craftsmen (literally) and of mathematical thinking. The adventurous and experimental poetics of this ontology frames the work of many of the architects discussed in this book (companion architects in parentheses): Richard Blythe (Mark Burry), dRMM (Flores & Prats), CRAB studio (Cassandra Fahey), Minifie van Schaik Architects (TAKA), CZWG (MDMA) and Ushida Findlay (Sarah Calburn).

The Cathedral of Saint Peter of Beauvais, Beauvais, France, 1284
At 48 metres (157 feet) high, this was to be the tallest cathedral in France. The collapse of some bays in the choir during construction in 1284 ended this ambition and terminated the search for height in Gothic architecture.

Architect as Idea Generator

The third ontology is an inclusive one in which the tectonic is subordinated to the idea of the project, as in the idea of the archetype of any building type. It is characterised by a willingness to cross boundaries, to draw analogies from other fields, importing mental frames and 'blending' them into poetics that are not entailed to either of the other histories.[24] Rasmussen foreshadowed this collage approach – fully articulated by Rowe[25] – positing qualities that architects assemble around varying ideas of inhabitation. Rasmussen wrote of architecture as colour planes and discussed the use of tapestries to alter the acoustic quality of rooms. He described architecture thought of as carved out of solids, literally at first, as in cave dwellings, and later conceptually through the 'moulding' of vaults and domes, an architecture that finds its apogee in the two-thousand-year-old Hagia Sophia in Istanbul.[26]

Despite mud brick being the basic material used in the cradle of civilisation, the Middle East, bricks somehow do not attract ideologues. They are as softly morphable as Rasmussen argues them to be, and can shift from one poetics to another. Even Louis Kahn (1901–1974) ignored his own mythical postulation that 'the brick be allowed to be what it wants to be' by using steel reinforcement in the arches of the Institute of Technology in Ahmadabad – steel that is now bursting the arches as it rusts.[27] It is in this context that O'Donnell + Tuomey talk of weaving a brick curtain for the

Little Moreton Hall,
Cheshire, England,
1504–1610
The long gallery on the
third floor was added in the
mid-16th century, revealing
the pragmatic nature of the
architecture.

Saw Swee Hock Student Centre at the London School of Economics and Political Science (2014). They bring together one technology and another to create a new architectural idea with its own poetics.

The architects in this book who work in this realm (companion architects in parentheses) include: John Brown (The Urban Foundation), Peter Hogg + Toby Reed Architects (Konstantin Melnikov and Amanda Levete Architects), DSDHA (Lyons), m3architecture (SANAA), W Architects (Stefano Boeri), Kristin Green Architecture (Sarah Calburn), WOHA (Sauerbruch Hutton) and the already mentioned O'Donnell + Tuomey (Searle X Waldron Architecture).

Architecture's Relationship to the Pursuit of Knowledge in Other Fields

The basic position taken in this book is that architectural knowledge is furthered through designing and also by building buildings. While I argue that it is the case that good architecture is concerned with our most current

Isidore of Miletus and
Anthemius of Tralles,
Hagia Sophia, Istanbul,
537
The original dome was
too flat and collapsed in
an earthquake in 558. The
second, higher dome at
55 metres (180 feet) was
designed by Isidore the
Younger.

Laurence Wilfred
'Laurie' Baker,
Indian Coffee House,
Thiruvananthapuram,
India, 1958
Laurie Baker used curved
masonry walls to amplify the
structural strength of bricks
and for their spatial effects,
designing many low-cost
buildings.

understandings of the universe and its make-up, architects contribute by
reflecting or directing social awareness through creating buildings that
have a poetic legibility, a readability. Just as in other fields, knowledge is
tested and disputed, most fruitfully when three substantive positions are
being argued for. Architects differ in their approaches to establishing the
poetics that frame their designing, negotiating between the three histories
outlined here. What they owe to other fields of knowledge is the conscious
understanding of how they design, how they establish the poetics of the
platforms from which they launch their designing. That is the thrust of the
following chapters of this book.

References

1. See IA Richards, *Practical Criticism: A Study of Literary Judgment* [1929], Harcourt Brace and World (New York), 1956.
2. Gaston Bachelard, *The Poetics of Space* [*La Poétique de l'espace*, 1957], translated by Maria Jolas, Beacon Press (Boston, MA), 1969 (first published in English in 1964 with the subtitle: *The Classic Look at How We Experience Intimate Places*).
3. 'Nests', Bachelard 1969, p 90; 'Drawers, Chests and Wardrobes', Bachelard 1969, p 74.
4. See Thomas L Schumacher, *The Danteum*, Princeton Architectural Press (New York), 1985.
5. Bachelard 1969, p 17.
6. See Christian Norberg-Schulz, *Intentions in Architecture*, The MIT Press (Cambridge, MA), 1963; Juhani Pallasmaa, *The Eyes of the Skin: Architecture and the Senses*, Wiley (Chichester), 2005.
7. See Trevor Garnham, *Melsetter House, Architecture in Detail*, Phaidon Press (London), 1993, and WR Lethaby, *Architecture, Nature and Magic* [1928; revised version of *Architecture, Mysticism and Myth*, 1892], Gerald Chatsworth & Co (London), 1956.
8. Steen Eiler Rasmussen, *Experiencing Architecture* [1959], The MIT Press (Cambridge, MA), 1964.
9. Colin Rowe, *The Architecture of Good Intentions*, Academy Editions (London), 1994.
10. Kenneth Frampton, *Studies in Tectonic Culture*, The MIT Press (Cambridge, MA and London), 1995.
11. Dalibor Vesely, *Architecture in the Age of Divided Representation: The Question of Creativity in the Shadow of Production*, The MIT Press (Cambridge, MA), 2004.
12. Leon van Schaik, *Spatial Intelligence: New Futures for Architecture*, Wiley (Chichester), 2008.
13. See Alberto Manguel, *The Library at Night*, Yale University Press (New Haven, CT), 2008.
14. Lethaby [1928] 1956, passim.
15. Clare W Graves, cited in Don Edward Beck and Christopher C Cowan, *Spiral Dynamics: Mastering Values, Leadership, and Change – Exploring the New Science of Memetics*, Blackwell (Business) (Cambridge, MA, and Oxford), 1996, p 28: 'Briefly what I am proposing is that the psychology of the mature human being is an unfolding, emergent, oscillating, spiraling process marked by progressive

subordination of older, lower-order behaviour systems to newer, higher-order systems as man's existential problems change.'

16. See Marshall McLuhan, *The Gutenberg Galaxy*, Routledge & Kegan Paul (London), 1967.

17. See Thomas Rowlandson and August[us] Pugin, *Weltstadt London von 1808–1810* [*The Microcosm of London*, 1808–1810], Harenberg (Dortmund), 1981 (facsimile edition).

18. See Frampton 1995 and Joseph Rykwert, *On Adam's House in Paradise: The Idea of the Primitive Hut in Architectural History*, Museum of Modern Art (New York), 1972.

19. The opening lines of Jean-Jacques Rousseau, *Of The Social Contract, Or Principles of Political Right* [*Du contrat social ou Principes du droit politique*], 1762.

20. See Erving Goffman, *Asylums*, Pelican (London), 1961, p 159.

21. See Aldo Rossi, *The Architecture of the City* [*L'architettura della città*, 1966], translated by Diane Ghirardo and Joan Ockman, The MIT Press (Cambridge, MA and London), 1982, and Aldo Rossi, *A Scientific Autobiography* [*Autobiografia scientifica*, 1981], translated by Lawrence Venuti, The MIT Press (Cambridge, MA and London), 1982.

22. See Harry Francis Mallgrave, *Gottfried Semper: Architect of the Nineteenth Century*, Yale University Press (New Haven, CT and London), 1996.

23. See Colin Rowe, *The Mathematics of the Ideal Villa and Other Essays*, The MIT Press (Cambridge, MA and London), 1976.

24. Mark Turner, *The Origin of Ideas: Blending, Creativity, and the Human Spark*, Oxford University Press (Oxford), 2014.

25. Colin Rowe and Fred Koetter, *Collage City*, The MIT Press (Cambridge, MA and London), 1978.

26. Rasmussen [1959] 1964, in particular the following chapters: 'IV: Architecture Experienced as Color Planes' (pp 83–104); 'Hearing Architecture' (pp 224–40); 'I: Basic Observations' (pp 9–34); 'II: Solids and Cavities in Architecture' (pp 35–55); 'III: Contrasting Effects of Solids and Cavities' (pp 56–82).

27. An apocryphal quote passed from teacher to teacher, recorded in one version in the documentary film by Nathaniel Kahn, *My Architect: A Son's Journey*, 2003.

Making Home

'Making home' is the fundamental basis of architecture. As in other fields of human endeavour – music, literature, sport, cooking – there is a continuum between what people do every day and what the most skilled professionals do. Economists argue that all of industry is outsourced domestic activity. If architecture is the elite expression of everyday acts of domesticating the world, then it is no more elite than is the opera singer or pop star we admire as we sing in the shower, the football star we think of as we kick a ball with our children, or the famous chef whose risotto we attempt to replicate at home. The architecture of making home, when understood, enables everyone to engage knowledgeably in the continuum of spatial thinking. Here is a range of exemplars that reveal architects working through differing poetic thresholds to create accessible architecture.

Feary + Heron, Plant
Room, Eagles Nest,
Zennor, Cornwall,
ongoing

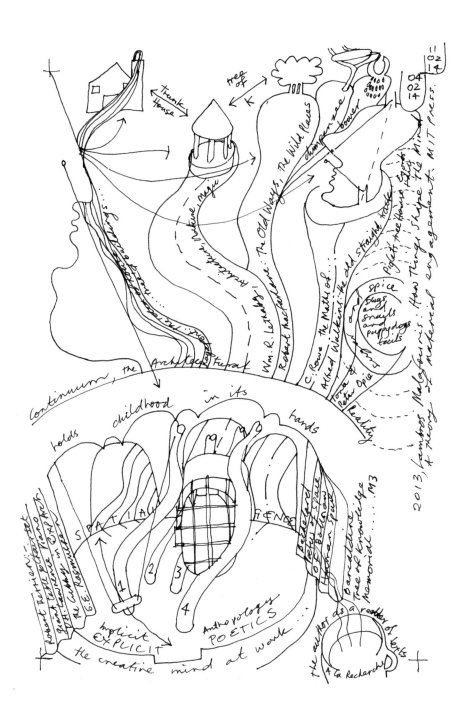

Trunk House

tree of K.

...shining through...

Architexture: Nature magic

Wm. R. Lethaby: 'Architecture, Mysticism and Myth'

Robert Macfarlane: The Old Ways, The Wild Places

C. Rowe the Mathis of...

Alfred Watkins: the old straight track

Iona + Peter Opie

Reality

champion zee

bower

spice slugs and snails and puppy dogs tails

Piglet the Hundred Acres wood

04 02 14

02 14

2013 Lambros Malafouris: How Things Shape the Mind a theory of material engagement MIT press.

Continuum, the Architectural

childhood in its hands

holds

SPATIAL

FIENDS

1 2 3 4

Robert Venturi: et
Robert Stern: et Hans
Grave Stern: in Oxford
17th century Ox...
R.E. Rosenweig

Implicit EXPLICIT

Anthropology POETICS

Bachelard
Poetics of Space
Bollingen
Tolkien Spirit

Bachelard
Tree of Knowledge
Memorial......M3

the creative mind at work

the author as a reader of texts

A la Recherché

Treehouse, Hobart, Tasmania, Australia

Richard Blythe, 2013

Architect and educator (Dean of Architecture and Design at RMIT) Richard Blythe, like Anaximander the Greek philosopher, argues that the making of a model precedes thinking about meaning in designing. Here Blythe uses mathematics to create a model and think that through into an architecture that does not symbolise an idea.

What are architecture's beginnings? This question haunts every consideration of the nature of architecture, its particular reality: what differentiates it from unselfconscious building.[1] To grasp the creative mind at work, consider the architect as a reader of texts, using 'texts' as a term that denotes what has been read by a particular architect; consider 'to read' as an expression for what has been absorbed from the culture the architect inhabits. Consider also the human capabilities or 'human-givens' that the architect brings to that reading.[2] These givens are better and better described by science,[3] have evolved over millennia and we all share them. Readings however are specific to every individual and if we want to understand a work of architecture we have to map the readings of its architects. That is why ontologies in architecture are so hotly disputed. Does architecture begin in a cave, when stones and boulders are rolled into a circle around a fire and sleeping platforms are carved into the softer flanks? Does it begin when branches or fronds are stacked against the trunk of a tree to make a circle of shelter? Or does it begin when saplings are bowed down into an arc and green wands of growth are woven between them?

Probably we cannot know, because while archaeology unearths the things that have shaped our minds,[4] it barely hints at the spaces that have shaped our spatial intelligence.[5] We could explore these old disputes, but best begin with a work of architecture: consider a treehouse designed and built for his two daughters by architect Richard Blythe. As we examine his drawings we discern the specific intelligence he brings to bear, what he is reading, and we see what readings he avoids.

Leon van Schaik, research ideogram, 11 February 2014
Drawn at the conclusion of researching the project.

Note how sparse and factual the drawing is. First Richard measures up a copse of trees in a steep gulley along the bottom boundary of his site. He has a section in mind, he has selected a level for the treehouse floor, and he

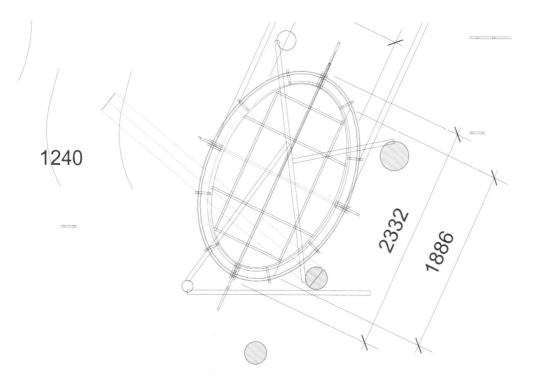

1240

2332

1886

measures the tree trunks at this level. Three substantial trees on the closer bank are shaded in grey. One of these leans across the gulley in a trajectory shown here in plan – a long rectangle running to the lower left. Two others, more slender, further into the stream, are drawn as hollow circles. The limits of the canopies above are borne in mind. Between the trunks Richard strikes an axis parallel to the line of the stream, a line that bisects the space defined by the trunks. This is an act as old as our first attempts to understand the universe. Sketching in this space, his hand brings an ellipse to mind, an instinctive nesting form derived from our even more ancient habits of mind, and he anchors this to the axis. We see this floating easily in the copse. We see it tested for size. Is it habitable? Yes it is! The architectural idea has arrived.

Now notice the traces of the construction idea: four thin rectangles depict temporary scaffolding bolted to the trunks. One pole spans between the leaning (grey) trunk and its (clear) opposite number. Three others seek to brace this scaffold and form a platform on which the ellipse can rest. But this is not the structure. If it were – thinks Richard – this would be the treehouse

Richard Blythe, Treehouse,
Hobart, Tasmania,
Australia, 2013
The oval of the treehouse
(photographed in 2014)
nestles between the trunks
of the trees – two hollow
circles to the left, three
shaded circles to the right.

he could have made as a raw boy, nailed inexpertly into the tree trunks, soon ripped apart by the movement of the trees. The ellipse must hang between the trunks. He seeks out tethering points: the ellipse will be hung on chains, more docked in the space formed by the trees than forcing them to become the structure. As the axis bisects the space, it bisects the ellipse, and it suggests a grid that forms the hardwood base platform of the treehouse. By now it is a hanging structure, much as the basket hangs from a hot-air

Richard Blythe, Treehouse,
Hobart, Tasmania,
Australia, 2013
The treehouse suspended
between the tree trunks.

balloon. This resonance is seized upon. The sides are hardwood strips woven between arced uprights, their arcs drawn freestanding to the left.

The elliptical base is built in the driveway nearby, rolled sideways between the tree trunks and then rotated on its axis and lowered onto the scaffolding. Chains are attached, the scaffold is removed. The geometry holds and facilitates the construction idea.

Richard Blythe, Treehouse, Hobart, Tasmania, Australia, 2013
The treehouse seen from the driveway where it was constructed before being rolled and then rotated into position.

Richard Blythe, Treehouse,
Hobart, Tasmania,
Australia, 2013
The abstract purity of the
elliptical form complements
the trees; it does not mimic
them symbolically.

Now consider what the architect did not do. If you do a search for treehouses, you will find hundreds of house ideas perched precariously on trees, usually destructively: these are not treehouses, they are concepts superposed onto trees. The idea of 'house' is childlike: a door mouth and two eye windows, a pitched hat roof, even sometimes a chimney too … These are uncomfortably forced marriages of two things that have their own separate beings. Richard is doing something very different. His finding of the geometry for his design is exactly that: a finding, conducted through sketching, not through imposing a preconceived form (circle, square, triangle).

Richard Blythe, Treehouse,
Hobart, Tasmania,
Australia, 2013
The treehouse is reached
by this rope ladder and
provisions are hauled up in
this basket.

Ellipses are strangely difficult to imagine, and disarmingly simple to construct.
Try this on a beach or on a lawn: push in a stake at the centre-point of the zone
that you want to occupy. Mark an axis along the long dimension of the zone
and pace out the furthest point that your ellipse will reach. Then take a pace

back from that edge, and plant a stake here. Then plant another stake on axis the same distance from the opposite edge. Take out the centre stake. Make a loop of string that goes from one of the new stakes to the farther edge of the axis. Using the first stake hooked into the loop, score along the ground, letting the string loop open out but keeping it taut to the two stakes in the ground. Slowly you draw this beautiful shape. And as you draw it you see the myriads of triangles that make the shape … Magic!

A few treehouses you will find when you search are geometric ideas, but these cling like limpets to a tree trunk, any tree trunk that has a columnar strength that the design can suborn, nailed and bolted violently into growing pith. Such designs are imposed, they have not been found by sketching particular trees, they are generic designs. Richard avoids the expected approach. Like a sailor understanding the wind and the waves, he has harnessed his trees to his purpose and they continue to move and to grow freely, while his basket 'holds childhood in its arms'.[6] These trees have not become 'structure' to an alien parasite, they lend the elliptical platform their strength: it is an idea their specificity has given rise to.

Here I think Richard is an architect in the ancient tradition of the geometers who measured and marked the passage of the sun through the seasons, and made structures like the 5,000-year-old Newgrange Passage Tomb in

Chimpanzees' nests, Kenya
There is a resonance between Richard Blythe's Treehouse and the elliptical form of the nests made by chimpanzees.

Companion to the Treehouse: Antoni Gaudí, Sagrada Família, Barcelona, 1883–2014
To help complete Gaudí's famous masterpiece, which has occupied numerous architects and craftsmen since his death in 1926, Mark Burry used mathematical modelling to draw out the underlying fractal geometries that Gaudí intuited. The cathedral has become a celebration of natural form.

County Meath, Ireland, which the sun at the winter solstice, and only then, penetrates. This treehouse, however humbly, is party to a poetics of the universe, uncovering, revealing and obeying its laws. But the architect also draws on ancient spatial thinking, still evident in the ellipses that chimpanzees make when building their nests in forest canopies.

WoodBlock House, London

de Rijke Marsh Morgan Architects (dRMM), 2013

The poetics of WoodBlock House is the result of many mental frames blending;
it is in conversation with the poetics of concrete and clay neighbours and thus
with other poles in the local culture. It speaks to international histories, to the
idea of 'house', and to the personal histories of client and architect.

Alex de Rijke (principal in the practice dRMM and Dean of Architecture at the
Royal College of Art, London) is fascinated by the act of building. This has its
roots deep within his experience. As a young man, he sent his mother away
on holiday, telling her he would put a new roof on her house by the time she
returned. When she did, and she opened the front door, there was no house
there. One thing had led to another as Alex unpicked the house, until a very
young relative reported to those waiting on the sidelines: 'There's no roof,
only sky, and everybody says "fucking …".'

Timber was the answer to most design questions, and to what Alex could
do. An engineer sized up the beams, these arrived and Alex looked at the
mass of wood, and knew that it was too much. He built what looked right,
and it was right.

Years later, as a director of dRMM, he designed a cross-laminated timber
(CLT) school sports hall. He describes how different this building site was
to others he had experienced, how the warm colours and sweet smells
of timber being worked in the warm dry atmosphere replaced the damp
and nostril-clogging dust of a cold concrete and masonry site. Timber has
become a driving fascination.

dRMM do use materials other than timber, seeking out their specific poetics.
The Tower of Love building (2012) at Blackpool is a wedding pavilion that –
in conversation with its beach location – twists its upper floor into a stalk
that eyeballs the famous Blackpool Tower. This is the favourite room for
marriage ceremonies. The tower is timber, but for the pavilion base dRMM
developed polished, Roman-style concrete bricks that used green glass and
brown glass from discarded wine and beer bottles as aggregate. These give
a flickering light akin to the rotating flashes from the myriads of mirror balls
inside the city's pleasure palaces.

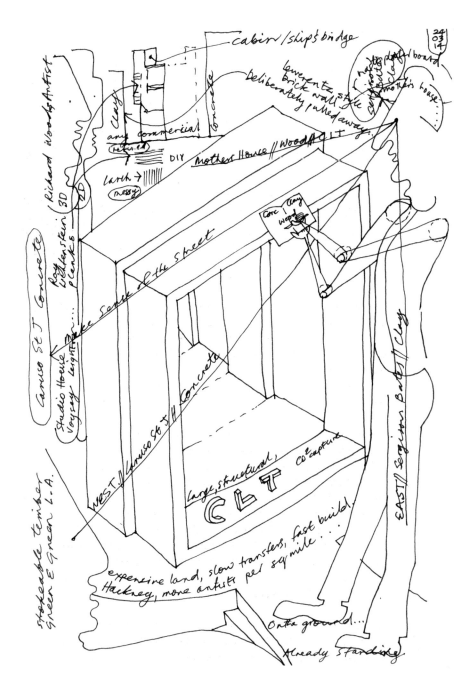

cabin / ships bridge

24/03/14

Lorenetz style brick wall. Deliberately pulled away.

Richard Woods/Artist

Clay concrete

any commercial natural

DIY   Mothers House // Wood // CLT

Larch → messy

2D

Rogleustein 3D planks

Carnso St // Concrete

Studio House Voysey Lightness

See sense of the street

Conc Clay
Wood

Large, structural, CLT   CO₂ capture

WEST // Carnso St // Concrete

EAST // Bequine Butts // Clay

expensive land, slow transfers, fast build. Hackney, more artists per sq mile . . .

Stackable timber Green & Green L.A.

On the ground . . .

Already standing.

dRMM, Tower of Love,
Blackpool, 2012
The Tower window of the
marriage celebration chapel
cranes its neck to focus on
the Blackpool Tower.

Yet, Alex remarked in April 2013 as he showed me dRMM's latest CLT
building, how much happier everyone working with timber was. This project
is a studio house in the 'any commercial/residential' zone of the London
borough of Hackney, formerly filled with small factories and now with a
greater concentration of artists than any other part of the city. Land has
become very expensive, and purchasing and planning processes are slow. To
be affordable, the build had to be fast and allow for some self-finishing.

Richard Woods, an artist who works in wood, and his wife Jess Espagnol,
knew of CLT construction through previous art installation collaborations with
dRMM. For the clients, parts of the design are very pragmatic. There had to
be a large ground-floor studio space accessible from the street. A residential
area above had to have a totally separate entrance. The architectural response
makes use of the long north–south-running rectangle of the site, using
the dual-aspect orientation for work and living respectively. A series of CLT
frames that nest within each other form the walls, the floors, the ceilings and
the roof structure. The large prefabricated frames were craned into place and
fixed in a very short time span, creating a warm dry working environment for
the crafting of the stairs and the installing of glazing and secondary services.

Leon van Schaik, research
ideogram, 24 March 2014
Drawn at the conclusion of
researching the project.

Then more layered thinking enters the picture. The artist makes what are
often described as Pop, Roy Lichtenstein-like stencilled planks of painted
plywood. Laid horizontally, these sheath the upper floors and form the

treads and risers of the staircase, almost advertising the 'trade' undertaken here, but also marking the building with the deliberate confusion between painting, sculpting and making furniture that is the artist's major project. The artist clad the lower floors vertically in rough-hewn, unpainted larch planks, blurring the functional actuality behind by deliberately confusing the separation between studio and house but suggesting a rustic base/piano nobile distinction.

dRMM, WoodBlock House, London, 2013
Cross section showing the offset to the left that provides separate ground-level access to the studio yard.

Here we encounter a process of naming, each act of naming creating a mental holding frame that enables the architect and his client to fuse disparate ideas into the new idea that is this house. The larch says 'timber' unselfconsciously. The stencilled boards ask 'Is a plank a plank?' The process intensifies.

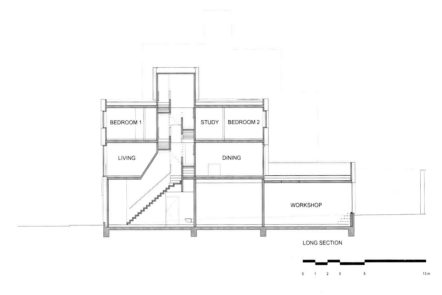

BEDROOM 1   STUDY BEDROOM 2

LIVING   DINING

WORKSHOP

LONG SECTION

0 1 2 3   5   10 m

dRMM, WoodBlock House,
London, 2013
The south elevation with
living room opening onto
the deck over the studio,
bedrooms above. Note the
timber to each side of the
large glazed door: these are
the CLT frames that provide
structure, insulation and self-
finish. The coloured cladding
above is timber grain painted
by the artist.

dRMM, WoodBlock House,
London, 2013
Long section showing the
separate stair to the dwelling
and the studio below.

To the west is a new masonry studio house – and the studio house as a type
has already been 'named'. It was designed by architects Sergison Bates.
Naming the frames positions the West in a tradition of works by that firm.
They are specialists in masonry, itself a frame onto the element of Clay. The
boundary wall of this house is roughly cement-bagged masonry, and we
might leave it there on first sight, but for its crafting and the play of light
upon it, which reminded Alex of the humble classical approach of Sigurd
Lewerentz (1885–1975) – another powerful cultural frame. Celebrating this,
the design pulls away, creating a side access to both entries and the rear
court. But the design also makes a new mental frame through the contrast
between the elements of Wood and Clay.

To the east is an empty site awaiting a studio house, the pair but not the
mirror to this one, and to the east again is the white (simulated concrete)
Coates House, home of the Caruso St John practice, high priests of Concrete:
four mental frames are jostling there, not including the frame that East could
be, and there is the newly charged frame of Concrete versus Wood (versus
Clay). Anyone of a certain generation will now hear the lyrics to Unite 4+2's
number-one hit single: 'The concrete and the clay beneath my feet begins to
crumble' – another frame, but a frame hinged from a previous generation's
experience, as none of the protagonists were there in 1965; let us say this is
a critic's frame? On the upper deck a wall of glass faces south. The windows

dRMM, WoodBlock House, London, 2013
View down the stairwell of the dwelling, showing how everything is made of cross-laminated timber (CLT), while the treads are covered with the artist's characteristic painted timber grain.

dRMM, WoodBlock House, London, 2013
The house, seen here between the clay brick Sergison Bates building to the right and the Caruso St John concrete office to the left, has a larch-clad base and a timber-grain-painted piano nobile.

have the push-out-and-slide mechanism of an automated train door, and close back behind the timber, concealing it. Two more named frames here: South in Northern Europe reeks of the longing for Italy that inspired the open loggias of architect Karl Friedrich Schinkel (1781–1841); the precision doors take us to the means of getting there.

Architects name in order to make mental frames that allow ideas to be brought together in new blends.[7] The quality of their blending depends on the acuteness of their naming, how well it captures the poetics of the instance that is being marshalled to join other instances in forging a new design.

Ground Floor

Second Floor

First Floor

Roof Floor

Plan labels: workshop; living; dining; terrace; bedroom 1; bedroom 2; study; bedroom 3; bedroom 4; studio; terrace; studio

Behind or beyond these framings lies the tale of the mother's house: that physically induced mental space that dwells on making buildings without the waste of flummery, using one material, one trade … and avoiding the cold, damp intractability of so many building processes. There is the bigger frame of CO_2 capture, the possibility that using timber as the material with which our explosively growing cities are made could help combat climate change in the Anthropocene, the fact that in fires, by charring on its outer skin, CLT outperforms concrete, clay and steel.

A void, coiled through with a staircase that reveals the CLT structure of all floors and walls and panels with artist-stencilled plank treads, runs through

dRMM, WoodBlock House, London, 2013
Plans: ground floor showing the separate entrance to the dwelling and the studio reached along the offset access way; first floor showing living spaces and deck over studio; second floor showing the four bedrooms and the bathrooms; roof floor showing the 'captain's bridge' studio/reading room.

the house from the entry space at ground level to an arrival alcove with seat dividing a living room with a full-width dining-kitchen area opening onto a big deck. It goes on up through the landing and service rooms to two bedrooms facing south and two facing north, and on again to a tiny reading cabin with a ship's bridge view across the roofscape of clay Hackney. This void soars up as if to a roofless conclusion in the sky, while the packed bookshelf wall of the cabin speaks of solitary study, and the hatch-like windows invite you to step out and situate your contemplations across the world city and beyond its horizons.

Companion to WoodBlock House: Flores & Prats, House in a Suitcase, 1996
The house comes in two large trunks and unfolds out of them.

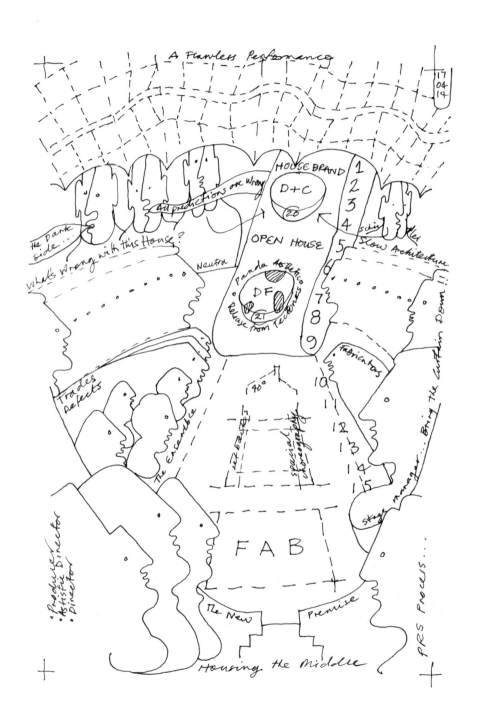

A Flawless Performance

17
04
14

HOUSE BRAND

All predictions are wrong

D+C
20

The Dark
Side...

What's Wrong with this House?

Neutra

OPEN HOUSE

Slow Architecture

1
2
3
4
5
6
7
8
9

Panda Aesthetics

D F
21

Release from Tectonics

Trades
Defects

Fabricators

10

The Ensemble

40°

Special Choreography

11

12
13
14
15

Stage manager

...Bring the Curtain Down!!

· Producer
· Artistic Director
· Director

FAB

The New

Premise

Housing the Middle

PRS PROCESS...

FAB house prototype, Calgary, Alberta, Canada

John Brown (housebrand), 2014

For architect John Brown (director of housebrand), this is not about a particular house but about reconceiving the suburban house. It is about ways of lightening what is pejoratively referred to as 'sprawl'. The project begins with the belief that good design can and should help everyone live well.

The nature of consciousness, the location of mind, how or where ideas originate – these framers of our search for meaning all elude definitive observation and description. There are 'plausible' accounts of how, after four million years of evolution, our consciousness began to change its nature about 50,000 years ago; of how we began to build mental frames that could carry entire worlds of experience into conversation with other such frames; and of how the frames we commonly use today, the calendar for instance, began to form around 5,000 years ago.[8] There are persuasive arguments about the social nature of and the persistence of consciousness, persuasive to some scientists at least.[9] Archaeology is now seen by some as research into the emergence of 'mind' as a relationship between humans and the material world.[10]

So surfacing evidence about how a design practice evolves is an activity that is difficult but also excitingly close to research into the origin of ideas. The Calgary practice of housebrand, of which John Brown is one of three directors, has an unusually clear agenda. Eschewing the heroics of formalist contemporary architecture (mental frame one in this argument), John Brown set out to lighten 'the dark side of the American dream', the vast tracts of suburbia that do not benefit from the application of architectural intelligence or spatial thinking, expertise from which only 3 to 8 per cent of houses or housing benefit (mental frame two).[11] The first move was to create a vertically and laterally integrated service joining up real estate, design (architectural and interior), construction and lifestyle merchandising (mental frame three). This had an immediate impact on the city: a ring of forty-year-old suburbs with housing stock ready for redevelopment became the locus of opportunity, as likely houses were identified, purchased, redesigned and furnished. Shown is a typical redesign: spatial flows have been created, underused half-basements have been brought into contact with the outside, thus releasing space to allow the carving out of larger rooms. A layered tectonic using everyday skills of tradesmen imparts a unified aesthetic.

Leon van Schaik, research ideogram, 17 April 2014 Drawn at the conclusion of researching the project.

Housebrand, Glendale
Residence, Calgary,
Alberta, Canada, 2013
The existing exterior above;
the renewed exterior below.

This approach to working changed the nature of the office. Formerly situated
over the lifestyle shop run by one of the directors, the office had had a small
reception area, a large directors' office and a large back office. Now the
directors moved into the back office and a reception lounge was formed,
becoming an extension of the shop. The potential clients were given the

major part of the space as they filled in questionnaires about their needs and desires, and options were negotiated.

Based on their burgeoning experience, the directors produced a best-selling book, *What's Wrong with this House?*,[12] and ran a series of open Saturdays in which they workshopped kitchens and bathrooms and space planning. Videos of these workshops reached hundreds of thousands of people. Meanwhile more than 2,500 Calgary clients benefited from refreshed houses decluttered and spatially and tectonically reorganised on principles learned from Richard Neutra (1892–1970) and Rudolph Schindler (1887–1953). Housebrand, purchasing houses, redesigning and reconstructing them using the same trade skills as mass builders, was reaching the upper echelons of those who were formerly unable to afford architectural services.

Housebrand, FAB house prototype, 2014
Drawing of moveable cupboard divider system.

This situation arose through the melding of the three mental frames listed above. Through practice it became a new mental frame (the fourth). It

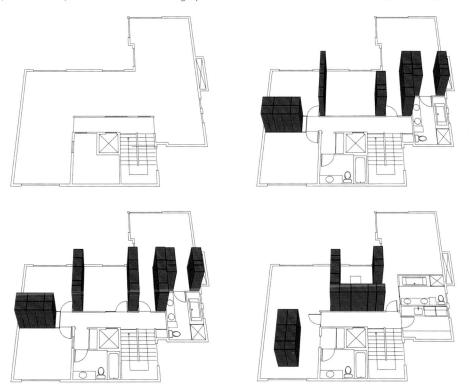

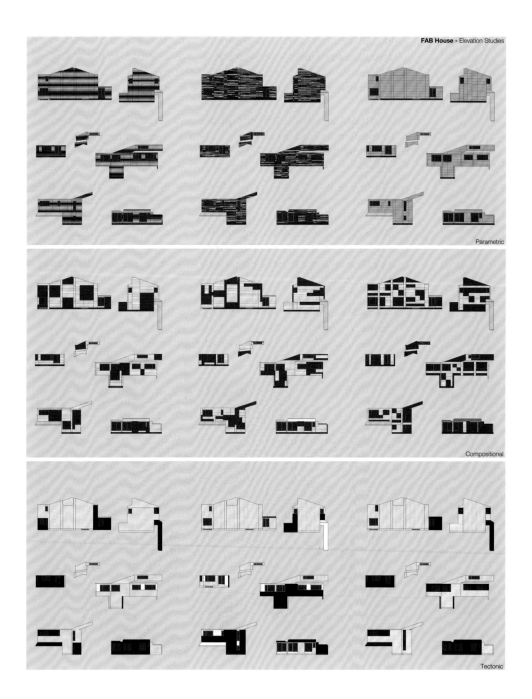

Parametric

Compositional

Tectonic

Housebrand, FAB house
prototype, 2014
Rendering showing the
development through
superimposition of the
panda facade in which the
markings do not coincide
with functions.

niggled that they were still not operating at the median of this market. After a decade of practising with this model, it also bothered John that early clients whose children had grown and whose parents had aged were presenting with the desire for a new house that suited their changed life circumstances.

John heard a mantra: 'All designs are predictions, and all predictions are wrong.' This he adopted as a fifth mental frame, and it drove him to a series of analyses. What kind of plans were they producing? What made them unsuited to the changing needs of families? What was hindering the move into a lower cost bracket? Two kinds of ideas emerged. The first examined stripping out those internal dividers that made the plans fixed. John was aware of 'long-life, loose-fit' designs in Europe, such as John Habraken's 1960s concept of 'supports' – base buildings containing un-fitted-out apartments.[13] But no one had applied this thinking to the suburbs before. In a sixth frame, John Brown came up with a system of cupboard dividers that could be reconfigured.

That drove another new idea: for the cupboards to be genuinely moveable, the services had to be rationalised. A vertical armature emerged, with horizontal arms. This concept separated the services from the carcass of

Housebrand, FAB house
prototype, 2014
Digital model of the services
armature of the prototype.

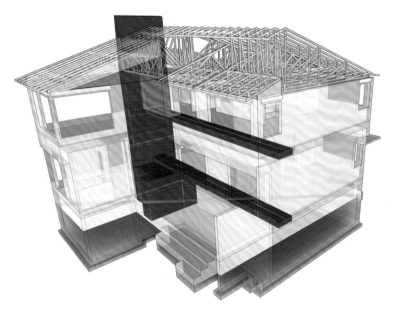

the house, and led to the idea that these could be fabricated off-site and assembled on site. This was the germ of a seventh mental frame: 'fabrication not construction'.

The analysis then moved into the three-dimensional form of the houses. A member of the team used a commercial software system to model the houses in paper cut-outs. This reduced the designs to paper skins without tectonic shifts. Noticing the abstractions of the facades, John mapped 18 of the built facades over each other and developed a composite that reminded everyone of the markings on a panda bear because the emphases no longer related to functional features of the exterior. This created the eighth mental frame: the release of the composition of facades from the tectonic language developed from Neutra and Schindler.

In turn, this changed the perception of the carcass of the house, which was now fully conceivable as a fabrication task, reinforcing the structure. In the minds of housebrand, Design and Construct died, and Design and Fabricate was born. This gave the project its initial name 'dFAB' (later 'FAB house'). Now a new mental frame (number nine) was grasped. A discussion between old friends, one a professor of theatre, another the CEO of an oil drilling company, revealed that the success of the latter, which worked on the principle of 'the flawless (if not perfect) performance', owed much to ideas drawn from theatrical practice. John's analysis had shown that there was a difficulty in completing projects. Fabrication could address many of the failings of trade interfaces that caused multitudes of tiny problems. But it dawned on him that housebrand could be seen as a company aiming for flawless performances, over and over again, as in the run of a play. One of the other directors was the producer, he was the artistic director, and the other was the executive director. There were many actors, but without a stage director and without rehearsals they were a loosely constituted team tackling every project afresh, not a performing ensemble making sure that everything was as the directors wanted it, over and over again, until completion.

Now housebrand is reconfigured as the studio for this ensemble. The first prototype of the FAB house is complete. There are three configurations: one square with an attached garage/multipurpose space, another handed version of this and the third being a narrow plan. Within the constraints of a minimum 40-degree pitch, they have stepped sections offering the effect of a loft space. The designing of each house holds the services armatures

Housebrand, FAB house prototype, 2014
Interior of the FAB house, with moveable closet prototypes.

in common, but its composition is determined in relation to orientation, specific site conditions, the location of surrounding houses, and the streetscape. The landscape is brought in by an urban farm specialist and is thus also fabricated. The median market has been reached with a flexible interior and a customised exterior.

John has mastered the art of identifying and crystallising mental frames in such a way that they can be brought together to create new frameworks for practice. This housebrand achieves within their overarching value system. Discarding normative tectonic aesthetics, the firm has created a new poetics. With this it can bring the benefits of architectural thinking to people who live out their version of the American Dream in its undervalued suburbs. The shifts in practice that brought housebrand to this position seem abrupt and mysterious until the mental frames that inform the practice's thinking is analysed. What happens at housebrand is aligned to the way in which archaeologists believe 'mind' is created: interactions between us and the material world we engage with advanced thinking.

Companion to FAB house prototype: The Urban Foundation, self-build house, Khutsong, South Africa, early 1980s
Within a prescribed framework, these houses were designed by their owner–builders, defying received taste, but signalling home.

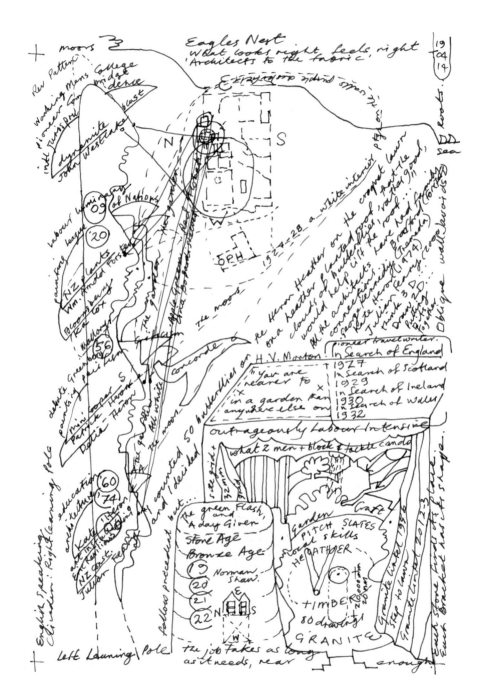

Eagles Nest
What looks right, feels right
'Architects to the fabric'

19
04
14

moors

N
S
W

S.P.H

1927-28 a wide interval

"You are nearer to in a garden than anywhere else on"

H.V. Morton

pioneer travel writer.
In Search of England
1927
In Search of Scotland
1929
In Search of Ireland
1930
In Search of Wales
1932

outrageously Labour Intensive
what 2 men + block & tackle can do

The green Flash, And a day Given

Stone Age
Bronze Age
19
20
21
22

Norman Shaw.

N   S
E
W

Garden
Craft
PITCH SLATES
social skills
HEATHER
TIMBER
80 drawings
GRANITE

Granite Lintel 1956
Step to lawn
Granite Lintel 20.12.3

The job takes as long as it needs, near   enough

Left Leaning Pole

Remodelling and new Plant Room at Eagle's Nest, Zennor, Cornwall, England

Feary + Heron, ongoing

Eagle's Nest has grown organically as generations have added to it, but its creative and technical continuities commenced with a creative rupture. A great house and garden develops through time. Here is the most recent addition to this house and garden, crafted by architect Julian Feary of Feary + Heron.

Writing of the ancient world, Mary Beard has commented that we approach it as if on a journey to a castle on the horizon, becoming more confident of our understandings of its detail until we are upon it, when we discover that there is a deep chasm between us and its already open doors.[14] We cannot readily enter into the values or mores through the doors. As we peer at old photographs or read inscriptions in churchyards, we are struck simultaneously by seeming continuities and the unbridgeable distances between recent generations, indeed between ourselves as we were and as we have now become, and think we will be. So we construct stories, tell them to ourselves, share them in our families, with our friends, and occasionally have them contradicted or corrected by biographers, who however build descriptions that nest on descriptions in a wavering approximation to documentary evidence and recorded memory.

Human places begin when someone pegs a stake into the ground. Without exception, places are seeded by such an

John Westlake, Eagle's Nest, Zennor, Cornwall, England, 1880s
View to the gables (added in 1890) from across the croquet lawn.

Leon van Schaik, research ideogram, 19 April 2014
Drawn at the conclusion of researching the project.

act. What we do not fully appreciate is that what is seeded is far more than a material fact; every stake is a viral seeding of the culture that caused it to be hammered in. Take Eagle's Nest at Zennor in Cornwall, a house and garden on a spur jutting out from upland moors over the ancient skirt of fields and farms bounded by stone walls. Here in the 1880s on a site between commons and farms, the Cornish-born Chelsea resident John Westlake (1828–1913), pioneering Professor of International Law at Cambridge University and one of the founders of the Working Men's College in London, built a country house in the western half of a rectangular field subdivided into stone-walled chambers around large granite boulders.

This act was a complex one. It was a coming home for a successful man, a man who defined the nature of peace between nations, who used the new invention, dynamite (1867), to form a lawn and speed up access to the site for the local stonemasons. He admired the skills of these men who split granite on the Tors above the house, using ancient techniques. Later, when the masons had crafted the big, almost cubic, house, Westlake set a large, cut stone inscribed in their honour adjacent to the Tor from which the stone was taken. The house was triple-fronted to the south, as was the pre-existing smaller Tregerthen Cottage built (possibly on the site of a shelter) by the Reverend Patten in 1849. In 1876 Westlake extended the house to the west to form the four principal rooms, adding in 1890 new gables: a larger one to the north partnered unequally the one based on the pre-existing house. Both gables faced the croquet lawn and the views to the sea across the farms below. Generous to his neighbours, in the hot summers of the late 19th century he gave garden parties on the lawn, inviting them all.

In his circle and that of Alice, his wife, was the art critic and social reformer John Ruskin, who for a while taught at the Working Men's College; and the suffragette Millicent Fawcett was a house guest. The neighbouring Old Poor House briefly belonged to the garden designer Gertrude Jekyll. The Liberal Unionist politician Hugh Arnold-Forster was also an acquaintance, and in 1920 the house passed to the latter's son, William Edward Arnold-Forster, the

George Kennedy, archway at Eagle's Nest, Zennor, Cornwall, England, 1927–8
The house seen from the granite boulders that form the rooms of the garden. The gabled extension at right angles to the house has an archway below the bathroom it provided at first-floor level. The half-gable window gives light to the kitchen Kate Heron added to William Edward Arnold-Forster's studio beyond.

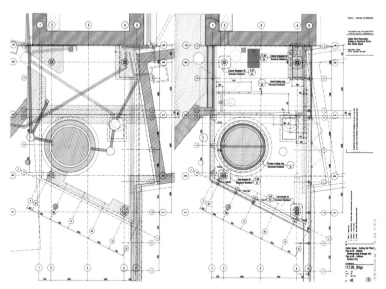

Feary + Heron, Plant
Room, Eagle's Nest,
Zennor, Cornwall,
England, ongoing
Plan of the Plant Room
showing the septic tank
(large light blue circle), the
timber screen (green line)
and the column bases (circles
with bolt-hole collars, two at
the top, three at the bottom,
two of which share an
elongated plate).

'Labour Luminary' active with the League of Nations, an avid gardener and a painter (member of the St Ives Society of Artists) who had studied at the Slade School of Art. He and his wife Ka Cox – who had been a lover to the poet Rupert Brooke and who counted the writer Virginia Woolf as a friend – planted out the gardens, reinforcing the rooms made by the remnant stone walls and granite boulders. Ruth Mallory, the widow of the mountaineer George Mallory, whom Arnold-Foster married after Ka Cox died, also worked on the garden, adding beds of lilies. On a childhood visit to the house over the winter of 1927–8, the future artist Patrick Heron saw the new planting. Arnold-Foster built a studio with north light to the rear of the house using an architect from Bradford (the weaving city that was the home to his family's industries); and he employed George Kennedy (an architect inspired by Richard Norman Shaw, who was related to a family in one of the farms below) to construct in granite an arched throughway with a bathroom above linking to the studio.

In 1956 Patrick Heron (like Arnold-Foster, a Slade-trained painter) and his wife Delia, retaining a flat in Chelsea, moved to the house with their young daughters Kate and Susannah. The house, garden and kitchen became the forge of remarkable artistic practice, the site of conversations between artist and landscape, and between artists and architects and critics (Patrick being a critic whose writing at first inspired and then enraged Clement Greenberg). The large white walls of the house were hung with the canvases produced by

Feary + Heron, Plant Room, Eagle's Nest, Zennor, Cornwall, England, ongoing
View along the timber screen to the courtyard beyond. The column is canted to preserve access to the folding doors to the left that open onto the tank-top deck.

Patrick, mostly in his studio in St Ives. The rooms of the garden hosted many weekend parties, and in summer the croquet on the lawn would be halted as Patrick enjoined his visitors to look for the green flash that would – if conditions were right (which they rarely were) – burst up out of the redness of the setting sun as if they were one of his paintings.

In 1974 Delia commissioned Kate Heron to convert the old studio and the offices linked at ground level to the arched throughway into a self-contained flat. Kate cleaned out the spaces, gave the white-painted studio a white lino floor, inserted a shower and WC under the main house bathroom, and created a galley kitchen with Lina Bo Bardi-inspired shelving across the window to hold a collection of lustreware crockery and pots and pans. Interested in the radical use of colour in her architecture, notably acid yellow in her London flat, Kate here elected to use that archetypal 1960s colour, Apple Green. In the studio a large red flokati rug surrounded by large red beanbags complemented this. It was like walking into a painting, and no paintings were hung in the space.

In 2000, Julian Feary, Kate's partner in architecture and in life, who had worked on large art projects with Patrick Heron, began the task of restoring Eagle's Nest. He saw this as an 'architect to the fabric' role, making the building true to itself and its history. Working with dedicated local craftsmen, rotting lintels and windows were replaced, floors restored, and insulation, double glazing and contemporary services and heating installed. Under the architect's observant eye a concrete lintel over the picture window inserted in the kitchen in the 1950s was replaced, using block and tackle and bulwarks of wood, to insert a granite piece intended for that purpose but used for decades as a step to the lawn after lifting it into place defeated those earlier builders.

Feary + Heron, Plant Room, Eagle's Nest, Zennor, Cornwall, England, ongoing
Detail of the timber screen fixing to the granite outcrop. The technique of drilling a hole and then cementing in a support is traditional.

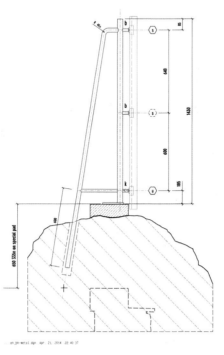

The studio flat is soon to be restored, but to allow that the boiler installed there needed a new home. Here Kate and Julian decided to make a garden store, outside lavatory and Plant Room behind the studio, removing a blockwork screen wall and turning the water tank top into a large deck. Here Julian, having restored the granitic nature of the site by removing the blockwork wall,

Feary + Heron, Plant
Room, Eagle's Nest,
Zennor, Cornwall,
England, ongoing
The Plant Room with its
slanting column seen from
the sheltered courtyard,
one of the rooms that the
boulders delineate.

decided to make the new extension using a 32-millimetre (1¼-inch) timber
screening module. His design had to mesh this with the siting of a 12-metre-
(40-foot-) deep septic tank in the only available space left after mapping the
pipes to and from this and to and from the boiler around the existing rocks and
rhododendrons.

Five highly engineered columns on four bases support a plywood laminated
tray, which is bolted in place with red brackets and holding the soil for a
heather-covered roof, a choice inspired when Julian saw on a late summer
day fifty or more butterflies on the heather on the lawn – twenty per square
metre, he calculated – and he thought that 'clouds of butterflies would help
lift this roof'. The timber ceiling and timber columns are a warm honey colour,
in contrast to the prevailing grey of the granite masonry and the boulders.
Deliberately Julian had his meticulously purposeful brackets for the tray and
the screen supports, and for the column bases and heads, made by local
metalwork firms. One column, sharing a base with another, cants to make
way for the pathway through the space.

The screen cuts across the tank and ends on a granite outcrop in a way that
is reminiscent of Álvaro Siza's dictum: 'Architecture is geometry and nature is
nature, so we have to look for the contact point.'[15] And express that contact

with a clear distinction, as Julian does when the screen, concrete base, galvanised supports and timber slats adroitly meet a granite boulder.

For several generations this sparse granitic landscape has attracted people who think and make, and who embrace a mutual esteem between thinking and making: international jurists, feminists, painters, gardeners and architects. Today, it is much less favoured as a cultural pole than, for instance, Cliveden – that great mid-19th-century house perched on a wooded cliff over the Thames valley – a house built on foundations laid by the corrupt 17th-century Duke of Buckingham, the king's favourite, killed by assassins; site of the first performance of the patriotic anthem *Rule, Britannia!*; home to the redoubtable socialite Nancy Astor in the first three decades of the 20th century.[16] Another stake in the culture that is English. No architecture is free of associations. Somehow the austerity of Cornwall attracted rebellious thinkers. And making the granitic landscape of Eagle's Nest habitable, as in the new courtyard behind the timber screen that extends into the granite from the Plant Room, brings into being a poetics that resonates with the thinking of Ars Povera – the art that arises from and celebrates minimal resources – anywhere, be it Portugal with Álvaro Siza or the raked gardens of Japan.[17]

Companion to Eagle's Nest: William Richard Lethaby, Melsetter House, Hoy, Orkney, Scotland, late 1890s
Lethaby embellished and extended the original house, giving it a new and romantic history.

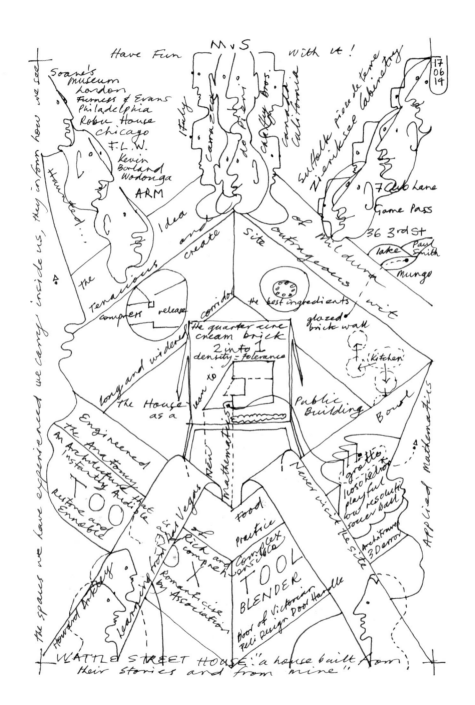

Wattle Avenue House, Mildura, Victoria, Australia

Minifie van Schaik Architects (MvS), 2012

In this project, architect Jan van Schaik builds civic consciousness in a remote regional centre. A pre-existing house is retained as an ennobled vernacular, while an annexe uses new mathematical forms. A combination of wit and regional cosmopolitanism produces a new crystallisation of the underlying poetics of Mildura.

Historically the house has served public functions. As ancient epics recount, for centuries the hall was a gathering place for communities, the family and their most important guests seated on a dais, privacy provided by mezzanine platforms and tapestries (such as the arras behind which Polonius hides to eavesdrop in Shakespeare's *Hamlet*).[18] Scholars have mapped the slow emergence of functionally different rooms, and – most importantly for our contemporary notion of the house – of the corridor.[19] The circumstances surrounding the Wattle Avenue House by Minifie van Schaik Architects (MvS) give this project an unusual civic poetics. Here the house as public building returns – partly socially, as a place in which a celebrity chef entertains, and partly as an expression of civic ambition. The house is freighted with the ambition of a handful of families intent on creating an independent regional culture and cuisine centred on the special characteristics of a multicultural (Anglo-Calabrian-Indo-Chinese) Australian city of sixty thousand people, centre of the irrigated desert that is the continent's 'food bowl'.

Before you dismiss this ambition on the grounds of the small scale of its population, consider the achievements of Columbus, Indiana, a city of the same scale. Columbus is the home of the engine manufacturing firm Cummins, and generations of the family who founded this company have had a passion for good architecture, starting in the 19th century in the centre of the town with their own Italianate villa complete with sunken garden. Concerned at the possible impact on the quality of the city of its rapid population expansion attendant on the growing demand for their engines during the Second World War, the Cummins family took the advice of the architect Eliel Saarinen, whom they had befriended when he was at Cranbrook Academy of Art, and set up a foundation that paid the architectural fees for any project that selected a designer from a panel set up by the trustees. This city now has 36 national monuments, including seminal

Leon van Schaik, research ideogram, 17 June 2014
Drawn at the conclusion of researching the project.

works by Robert Venturi, Harry Weese, Eliel Saarinen and his son Eero, and a lovely library – possibly the best IM Pei building anywhere.[20] So size does not matter. Ambition does.

Jan van Schaik, an architect who embraces the regional and provincial with a metropolitan zest, was fortunate to meet Stefano de Pieri in the gourmet restaurant Stefano had founded in the basement of the Grand Hotel overlooking the Murray River in Mildura. Here in the centre of the 'food bowl' Jan tasted a simple dish of fresh broad beans, a local cheese, a local olive oil and pasta made from local durum wheat with a matching local wine. An epiphany. The simple combination of 'slow' foods revealed the ambition of the chef – his drive to re-create value through the excellence of the products of the region, long denatured by subservience to globalised industrial food chains, retail and wholesale.[21] Appreciating Jan's surprised enthusiasm, Stefano took it upon himself to show the architect the region, and he and his wife Donata introduced him to the citizens who were behind the arts and writers' festivals in the city. In turn, Jan shared his enthusiasm for the architectural ambitions of the past, those examples of Victorian, Edwardian and Art Deco that had survived the debilitating internationalism of the second half of the 20th century.

Jan took his students to Mildura and ran studios on the urban potential of solar energy and the revamping of the irrigation system. So when Donata and Stefano decided to move closer to their burgeoning enterprises – brewery, winery, restaurant, café-gallery – they naturally sought Jan's advice. Together they toured the inner city suburbs until they settled upon an archetypal cream-brick, red-tile-roofed bungalow on a large plot opposite a convent school that Donata had attended. The Australian artist Howard Arkley captured the iconic nature of these houses in his paintings, exhibited at the Venice Biennale in 1999. This could be seen to be in the spirit of *Learning from Las Vegas* (1972), the Denise Scott Brown-initiated project in which she involved first Robert Venturi and later Steven Izenour.[22] This book had a particular resonance for Jan's architectural mentors in Melbourne, and an additional impact because his architect grandfather had been a close friend of Denise and her first husband

Howard Arkley, *Theatrical Facade*, 1996
Displayed in Arkley's one-man exhibition 'The Home Show' in the Australian Pavilion at the 1999 Venice Biennale, this synthetic polymer painting captured the poetics of the ubiquitous cream-brick houses of Australian suburbia.

Minifie van Schaik
Architects, Wattle Avenue
House, Mildura, Victoria,
Australia, 2012
The renovated cream-brick
house is to the right, the
new extension to the left.

Robert Scott Brown. Jan recalls however that his mentors at the Melbourne architecture practice ARM used the book to avoid the tyranny of 'context'. They advised him that, mentally at least, he should 'never visit the site' of a project. Context, they argued, was always an invention.

The option facing architect and client, an affordable one, was to demolish this house and begin again. But to do this would have been to succumb to the internationalising impulse that had rendered so much of the history of the city into an undistinguished pulp. So they very consciously developed a strategy that would frame the poetics of the suburban tide of the 1950s with the advanced architectural thinking of the award-winning practice MvS. This imbued the house with a civic mission: demonstrating how to preserve the dreams of the past and project a future vision. The house had to encompass a separate dwelling for Stefano's brother; two other bedrooms; a distinguished musician who spends six months of the year in Mildura; a large central

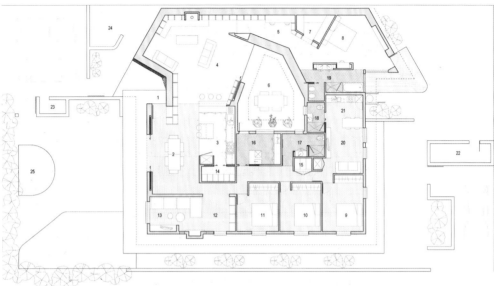

kitchen serving informal and formal dining functions; and a wing with a library, study spaces, dressing rooms and a master bedroom.

Jan, who aspires to 'an architecture that is rich and complex, instantly audible and comprehensible', matched his (as he puts it) 'tenacious and outrageous wit' to that of his clients and proposed the addition to the house of an over-scale lean-to. In the back of the architect's mind was a lean-to added to and eventually encompassing a caravan at a holiday site that he had visited. As he writes: 'The spaces we have experienced we carry inside us, they inform how we perceive space.'[23] Clad in humble cement-fibre sheeting, the extension resonates with the beach house vernacular of Australia, a vernacular also characterised by single-pitch roofs.

Where the extension clips onto the side of the gutted and restored brick house, a half-dome, looking like the impress of a low-resolution football, forms the generous entry portico. Jan writes that entries must be large and encourage lingering. The clients read this as an echo of the grotto in the wall of the convent opposite, and see it as signifying the sacredness of the threshold into the house (public) and the home (private) inside. Looking at its form, Jan's partner Paul Minifie, a champion of topographic mathematics

Minifie van Schaik Architects, Wattle Avenue House, Mildura, Victoria, Australia, 2012
Plan showing the 'U' of the pre-existing house below, the 'lean-to' above, the entry cove to the right and the courtyard to upper centre. The separable studio flat is to the left.

Minifie van Schaik Architects, Wattle Avenue House, Mildura, Victoria, Australia, 2012
A glazed brick wall wraps the new courtyard towards the living area, masking the master bedroom beyond.

in architecture, recognised – in an insight characteristic of his poetics – the imprint of an icosahedron, and indeed using this applied mathematical form resolves all of the junctions between new and old and allows for a consistent uncut tiling pattern for the fine Italian tiles that line its inner surface.

The new wing attaches to the two arms of the U-form plan of the house. The back arm, facing a large garden area, houses the separate flat, though – allowing other configurations – this is linked by a soundproof door to a corridor leading to two bedrooms and bathrooms in the main house. The rest of the plan is open around the kitchen, with the new reception room opening through a large sliding door to the hedged front lawn. A compression point between old and new (reminiscent of the compression

points in Frank Lloyd Wright's Robie House (1910) in Chicago, which Jan visited) releases into the clerestory-lit library and dining room, which in turn opens onto an internal courtyard incorporating the hollow of the original 'U'. A glazed brick wall curls around this and shelters the private quarters. The glazed faces of the bricks are patterned into a pixelated image of Lake Mungo in the desert, manipulated until it matched the striations on a favourite Paul Smith shirt owned by the architect. On facing walls hang paintings of the region that the clients have collected over the years.

In a sense the house is a poem concocted by clients and architect along the lines of the Surrealists' 'exquisite corpse' compositions, each party contributing independently. Each concatenation of memory and influence resonates down different tracks. For Donata and Stefano there are links to their connections to the Veneto region of Italy and to the great coastal cities of Australia, from which Mildura is almost equidistant. For Jan there is his personal history in space inflected by a family history in architecture and cabinetmaking stretching back through Melbourne, Johannesburg and London to 19th-century Holland. For Donata and Stefano and their allies there is the determined metropolitanism of the arts and cuisine that is being

Minifie van Schaik Architects, Wattle Avenue House, Mildura, Victoria, Australia, 2012
View across the formal reception area, with new opening to the lawn, and looking through the compression point between the old house in the foreground and the new living area beyond

Companion to Wattle
Avenue House: TAKA
(Alice Casey and Cian
Deegan), House 4,
Dublin, 2012
This house takes on
the general form of its
neighbours but enhances
every formal idea to create a
reverse archetype.

fostered. For Jan there are the influences of the Soane Museum (former
home of the architect Sir John Soane, 1753–1837) in London, the city in
which he was born; his love for the work of Furness & Evans in Philadelphia,
and particularly of the Library at the University of Pennsylvania (1890);
and his admiration of Kevin Borland's pioneering work at Clyde Cameron
College (1977) in the regional Australian city of Albury-Wodonga.[24] In
his full consciousness of the anatomy of his practice, the poetics of every
architectural move is accounted for.

References

1. See discussion in the Introduction.
2. See Leon van Schaik, *Spatial Intelligence: New Futures for Architecture*, Wiley (Chichester), 2008, and Joe Griffin and Ivan Tyrrell, *Human Givens: The New Approach to Emotional Health and Clear Thinking*, Human Givens Publishing (Chalvington, East Sussex), 2003.
3. Schaik 2008, pp 22–33.
4. See Lambros Malafouris, *How Things Shape the Mind: A Theory of Material Engagement*, The MIT Press (Cambridge, MA), 2013.
5. See Alfred Watkins, *The Old Straight Track*, Abacus (London), 1974.
6. Gaston Bachelard, *The Poetics of Space* [*La Poétique de l'espace*, 1957], translated by Maria Jolas, Beacon Press (Boston, MA), 1969, p 8: 'And the poet [Rainer Maria Rilke] well knows that the house holds childhood motionless "in its arms."'
7. See Mark Turner, *The Origin of Ideas: Blending, Creativity, and the Human Spark*, Oxford University Press (Oxford), 2014.
8. See Turner 2014.
9. See Robert Lanza and Bob Berman, *Biocentrism: How Life and Consciousness are the Keys to Understanding the True Nature of the Universe*, BenBella Books (Dallas, TX), 2009.
10. See Malafouris 2013.
11. See Robert Bruegmann, *Sprawl: A Compact History*, University of Chicago Press (Chicago, IL and London), 2005. Through historical and contemporary analysis this book counters received opinion about 'sprawl'.
12. See John Brown and Matthew North, *What's Wrong with this House? A Practical Guide to Finding a Well Designed Sustainable Home*, Slow Home Studio (Calgary), 2011.
13. See NJ Habraken, *Supports: An Alternative to Mass*

Housing [*De Dragers en de Mensen*, 1961], translated by B Valkenburg, Architectural Press (London), 1972.

14. Mary Beard, 'Laddish: *Nero* by Edward Champlin', *London Review of Books*, vol 26, no 17, 2 September 2004, pp 17–18.

15. Álvaro Siza on film, in the exhibition 'Sensing Spaces: Architecture Reimagined' (curated by Kate Goodwin), Royal Academy, London, 25 January to 5 April 2014.

16. See Schaik 2008, pp 131–2.

17. See Jerzy Grotowski and Eugenio Barba, *Towards a Poor Theatre*, Methuen Drama (London), 1994.

18. William Shakespeare, *Hamlet*, Act 3, Scene 4.

19. See Robin Evans, *Translations from Drawing to Building*, Architectural Association (London), 1997, p 77.

20. See Leon van Schaik, and Geoffrey London, *Procuring Innovative Architecture*, Routledge (London), 2010, pp 91–6.

21. Donata Carrazza and Stefano de Pieri, 'Beyond the Great Divide', in Peter Beilharz and Robert Manne (eds), *Reflected Light: La Trobe Essays*, Black Inc (Melbourne), 2006, pp 139–47.

22. See Denise Scott Brown and Robert Venturi, *Learning from Las Vegas*, The MIT Press, (Cambridge, MA), 1972.

23. See Jan van Schaik, unpublished PhD thesis, RMIT, Melbourne, 2015.

24. See Doug Evans, Huan Chen Borland and Conrad Hamann, *Kevin Borland: Architecture of the Heart*, RMIT Publishing (Melbourne), 2006.

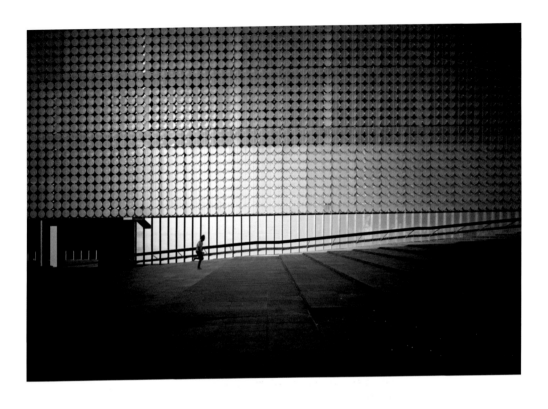

Feeding Body, Mind and Soul

Architecture that aims to change our understanding of how we live and adapt to emerging states of affairs in our world develops a poetics of its own. Such architecture has and promotes an ideal. Here poetics is forged around notions about waste-free living, sustainable energy use and recycling, the housing of art as an engine of meaning, the nurturing of a new economy, of new talent, and the housing of design education and research. Such architecture anticipates our dreams and it forms the carapaces of our desires before we have fully articulated them. Each project discussed sets itself up as a critique of prevailing ways of doing things. This poetics is created by thinking about where we ought to be rather than celebrating where we are.

Sean Godsell Architects,
RMIT Design Hub,
Melbourne, 2012

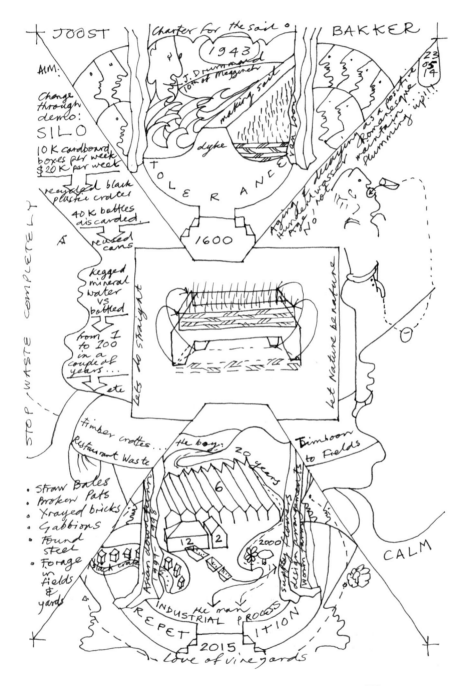

JOOST   Charter for the sail   BAKKER

1943

J. Drummond
10th of Megginch

AIM.

Change
through
demo:

SILO

10 K cardboard
boxes per week
$20 K per week

recycled black
plastic crates

40 K bottles
discarded

reused
cans

kegged
mineral
water
vs
bottled

from 1
to 200
in a
couple of
years...

etc

making sail

dyke

T O L E R A N C E

1600

Let's do straight

Let nature be nature

23
05
14

Ageing & decaying as a positive
thunderwassa Romanesque
plumming up!!

No!

STOP/WASTE COMPLETELY

timber crates... the boy...

Restaurant waste

20 years

Timboon
to fields

• Straw Bales
• Broken Pots
• Xrayed bricks
• Gabbions
• Found
  steel
• Forage
  in fields
  & yards

6

12   2

2000

black crates

the man

CALM

R E P E T   INDUSTRIAL PROCESS   I T I O N

2015

Love of vineyards

Melbourne Food and Wine Festival (MFWF)
Greenhouse, Melbourne

Joost Bakker, 2012

Can poetic sensibilities be passed from generation to generation? Inventor, designer, organic food and no-waste entrepreneur and advocate Joost Bakker has developed a poetics that integrates his beliefs and his innovations. A migrant to Australia, he retains a Dutch matter-of-fact-ness in his business ideas and in his designs.

The mystery of consciousness is being probed by every discipline, and here and there the fog lifts to reveal an aspect of its supposed mechanics, but only in the terms of each discipline's discourse. An abiding interest resides in how, and if at all, a generation can pass experience on to succeeding generations. Some argue that the genes – as in 'the selfish gene' that is supposed to govern our seemingly inherited notions of fairness[1] – can carry forward behavioural traits over millennia. The term 'meme' covers the belief that the mental frames of a culture are passed on from generation to generation in a process analogous to that in which our DNA passes on genetic information, and that passage is as susceptible to chance mutation and subsequent selection.

Professional disciplines construct their core mental frames through overt processes of formulating and testing the knowledge base they work from, acting as caretakers and innovators. But every one of us is subject to continuities that lie outside our disciplinary frames. I am only partly Dutch genetically, and have only ever visited the country briefly, but I am overtaken by a tide of emotion when I encounter a sea meadow with rows of trees, drainage channels and a dyke. There seems to be an inherited liking for this. There is quite a large Dutch expatriate community in Melbourne. They began arriving after the terrible floods of 1952, took one look at the river plane on which the city sits, and headed for the hills of the Dandenong Ranges. Among those that followed were a young Joost Bakker and his family. In those hills the family bought a house and land and set up a business growing flowers. They built a shed; that took two weeks. They imported a two-and-a-half-hectare (six-acre) greenhouse; that was erected in six weeks with absolutely no waste. They refurbished the house; skip after skip of rubbish was pulled out, it took 12 months. Fourteen-year-old Joost

Leon van Schaik, research ideogram, 23 May 2014
Drawn at the conclusion of researching the project.

marvelled at this, and relished the calm beauty of the greenhouse's regular
bays. To this day, that wonderment underpins his approach to designing.
The family businesses flourished; Joost set up selling the flowers, boxing
them and airfreighting them into Asia. He also ran a worm farm, using all
the waste organic matter. Look at all of this as a mental frame: it is a meme
for a certain kind of Dutchness.

Selling to Asia ended with the downturn of 1997–8, but Joost shared
premises with a mushroom provider, and visiting restaurateurs had taken to
buying flowers from him. Delivering flowers to their restaurants, Joost was
disturbed to see how artlessly they arranged the flowers; he showed them
how it could be done, and his design career began. But where it could have
become all theatre, Joost's practice grew from a well-documented meme:
'winning land from the sea; making nutrient rich soil from sand; egalitarian
cooperative networking to build and maintain dykes; rational geometry; let
nature be nature'.[2]

To this Joost added other frames also related to enriching the soil, and
thus the nutrient quality of that which is grown in it. He talks of John
Drummond, the 10th Baron of Megginch in Scotland (note the fascination
with continuity), who practised organic farming and wrote *Charter for the
Soil* (1943). Joost started to make installations, using found materials in
the main, and was then offered the opportunity to design a corporate tent
for the Macquarie Bank at the 2006 Melbourne Cup race. Here, amid the
froufrou of silk tenting, he used raw plywood and crates and put in place his
harvesting principles: all waste was collected and cycled back into the land
on his dairy farm and on the farms of his growing band of allies. The client
was horrified, but soon everyone was talking about it, and Joost was invited
back over the following years, until his attempt to extend the conversation by
building a glasshouse and growing provisions on site was vetoed. By now he
had the desire to build his ideas, and he began to build structures. The first,
at Federation Square (2008, assisted by architects Antarctica), was more a
skeleton than a building: exposed pipework showed every harvesting process
in action. More temporary pavilions followed.

The MFWF Greenhouse at Queensbridge Square on the Yarra River in
central Melbourne expressed many of Joost's core design beliefs. Although
temporary, it had the appearance of a structure that had been there and
would be there for a long time. A massive rectangular base made of
formaldehyde-free plywood, with a continuous trellis hung with myriads

Joost Bakker, MFWF Greenhouse, Melbourne, 2012
Although a temporary pavilion, the walls of steel mesh infilled with terracotta pots, the deep opening reveals lined in timber and the planted balustrade give the impression of permanence, such as eludes the curtain-walled towers behind.

of small terracotta pots, 'all four corners sturdily present', and three faces incised with three open doorways, supported a roof deck with wide planted balustrades. At one end he marshalled the drums and pipes of the recycling plant – all the processes open to view.

Joost's own home near the farms of his family (flowers) and of his wife (trees) epitomises his design approach: thick walls (straw bales here, but he also uses gabions filled with broken pots or bricks); large rectangular spaces; solid corners; external screens made from hundreds of pots of strawberries hung from steel reinforcing mesh; and an earth roof growing a wild meadow.

On a recent house, the meadow started with a layer of turf onto which Joost broadcast seeds foraged from the verges of a nearby railway track. Joost says that what you take away from the earth, you must add back – in this case literally by putting the earth covered by a house back onto the roof. The construction is economical. The spaces can thus be large and flowing, and the interiors have a cave-like equanimity of temperature, be it hot or cold outside. Everything is itself, there is no covering up, you can see what is what. The aim is more than recycling; it is the stopping of all waste.

Joost pursues his goals with a Dutch frankness. In Silo (2012), his inner-city café exemplar, there is a machine that dehydrates every scrap of waste and sends it out to the farms of his suppliers as compost. Showing the way to the lavatories, there is an image of a man drinking and pissing at the same time. The message is clear, no flummery. This is what happens. The Thames is said to pass through the human body seven times on its way to the sea; let's face up to this and deal with it! Let's no longer hide the realities. This is very Dutch: that way of doing things openly and ensuring that your diseconomies do not impinge on your neighbours.

The Dutch made their land over several centuries, cooperatively winning it from the sea. Their wealth was widely distributed – through the first stock exchange, because their

Joost Bakker, MFWF Greenhouse, Melbourne, 2012
Basil growing in drums of already used water. There is no such thing as waste in Joost Bakker's approach.

Antarctica Architects with Joost and Jennie Bakker, Monbulk House, Victoria, Australia, 2011
Thermally broken steel-frame windows here open into the plywood-lined interior of a bathroom. Steel frames carrying terracotta pots from which grow strawberries screen the insulated walls.

trade depended on what today we call crowd-sourcing – and their created land meant that there was no hereditary aristocracy that could dominate other classes.

There is in this meme an inbuilt optimism that people can change things. Joost's optimism relates to this. He knows that in his community things can be changed. In his own growing network, attitudes and practices change as people see how things can be done. At Silo, everything is made from found materials. Nothing arrives that needs to be disposed of or recycled through destruction. Milk comes in milk churns. Vegetables come in black plastic crates that make the journey over and over again. There are no bottles of mineral water. Joost demanded delivery in a keg. He was told this could not be done. He persuaded. It now is done, and restaurant after restaurant follows the example. If only the city council would more speedily

Antarctica Architects with Joost and Jennie Bakker, Monbulk House, Victoria, Australia, 2011
A chandelier made of scavenged rusted wire hangs in counterpoint to self-finished plywood and internal blockwork walls.

DAYLESFORD HOUSE
Currently under construction - due for completion October 2012

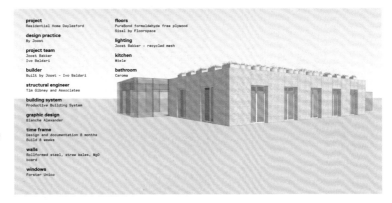

project Residential Home Daylesford	**floors** PureBond formaldehyde free plywood Sisal by Floorspace
design practice By Joost	**lighting** Joost Bakker - recycled mesh
project team Joost Bakker Ivo Baldari	**kitchen** Miele
builder Built by Joost - Ivo Baldari	**bathroom** Caroma
structural engineer Tim Gibney and Associates	
building system Productive Building System	
graphic design Blanche Alexander	
time frame Design and documentation 8 months Build 8 weeks	
walls Rollformed steel, straw bales, MgO board	
windows Forster Unico	

Joost Bakker, Daylesford House, Daylesford, Victoria, Australia, 2012
Design drawing showing the planted roof. The walls are straw bales in roll-formed steel frames, the interior is lined with self-finished magnesium oxide board.

facilitate plans to enable every restaurant to install dehydrators and so dispense with their rubbish bins!

Joost Bakker, Silo, Melbourne, 2012
Nothing arrives at Silo restaurant unless it can be returned or reused. Plastic crates used to transport vegetables line the ceiling. Diners sit at a central table in the kitchen.

Clearly though, Joost does not work in Holland. The mental frames of a cosmopolitan city intersect with the ancient Dutch meme, persistent though that is at a genetic level (the Dutch are the tallest people in the world and Joost, who has classic Dutch looks, jokes that his brother is the spitting image of Vincent van Gogh). These are the frames of Melbourne, a migrant city. More than 40 per cent of the population of Melbourne were born overseas. Joost has been supported and challenged by a migrant CEO who regarded him with intense suspicion, and then supported him. He was recognised and

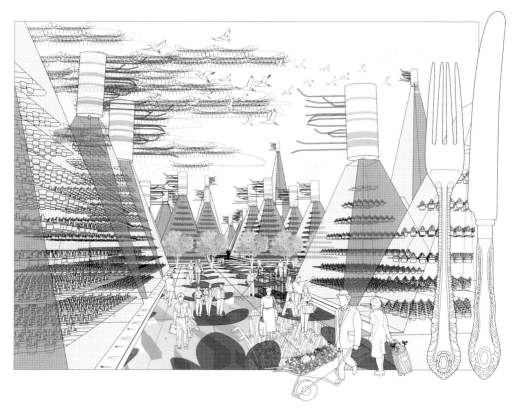

encouraged by the architect Nonda Katsalidis, whose 90-storey Eureka Tower (2006) rears up behind the MFWF Greenhouse and who arrived from Greece as a very young child to live in what is the world's second largest Greek city; by the young architects of Antarctica, who migrated from Western Australia and New Zealand; and by collaborators from every sector of his adopted city. Joost works with many different people, including architects, chefs and entrepreneurs, in Australia and elsewhere. His reach is international: in mid-2014 a Joost café opened in Brighton, England. His practice encompasses, and innovates in, many disciplines, working in their mental frames while the meme or gene of Dutch live-and-let-live tolerance, rational husbandry, calmness and entrepreneurship gives him the migrant's view of the edges of hosting memes and thus of opportunities that those embedded in their meme cannot see. This mixing of memes colours everything he touches.

Companion to MFWF Greenhouse: CJ Lim, illustration from *Food Parliament,* unpublished PhD thesis, RMIT, Melbourne, 2014
London reconceived as a food transparency city in which all food production takes place in full view of and as part of daily living.

't Raboes Project, Eemnes, Netherlands

Jo Van Den Berghe, 2013

Jo Van Den Berghe is what in Flanders is called a 'cultural architect', an ideas-driven sole practitioner, the kind that survive through their pursuit of ideal architectures; who risk all for their questing clients and who thus push the boundaries of the discipline. Here a poetics of what the architect calls 'inventio et executio' is revealed.

Designing is held within conversations. Conversations are engines for slow thinking.[3] Between the hand that draws and models and the eye that sees and recalls; between the library of peers and mentors of the designer and the designing hand/eye; between design partners who bring their own conversations into the conversation that shapes the design; between the designer and the clients, each bringing their 'little worlds' into play in the conversation that holds the designing.[4] 'The world is a den of thieves,' declares the principal character in Ingmar Bergman's 1982 film *Fanny and Alexander*, 'and night is falling. Let us celebrate our little world!'

The little world of this project concerns an estate made up of separate sites along the river Eems in Holland, each of which is the focus of acts of cultural entrepreneurship by the client and his family. His idea is to establish the civic spine of an ideal city – De Nieuwe Stad – of which this project, ''t Raboes', is the leisure–culture location. A site in Amersfoort contains housing and a restaurant and exhibition space designed by FAT Architecture. An old factory on another site has been converted into an incubator for young, green-economy enterprises, presaging a hoped-for new economy, De Nieuwe Economie. The client has a personal history in construction: 'I was born on a scaffold,' he likes to say. This project on the river Eems began with the purchase of a remote marina or yacht harbour on the flatlands of a polder reclaimed from the IJsselmeer lake. Founded by hippies, it had fallen into disreputable usage. Rescuing it for his home community, supplying covered moorings and workshops for his and other boats, and providing a 'gentleman's room' for himself, a 'boys' room' for his inventor and architect sons, and a painting studio for his daughter became the client's mission. At first the idea was to have four dwellings, one for each.

However, before building could begin there was the need for a raised platform of earth to lift the land above the 1953 flood level, for an avenue of lime

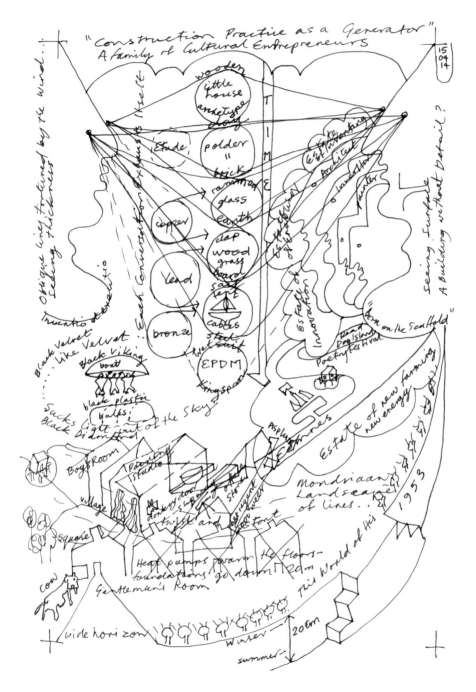

"Construction Practice as a Generator"
A family of Cultural Entrepreneurs

15/04/14

wooden
little house
anketype
glass

polder
"
brick
rammed
glass
earth
clay
wood
grass
board
salt
tent
cables
steel
surf
EPDM
Kingspan

Etude

copper

lead

bronze

estate
architect

painter

estate of innovation

estate of new farming
new energy

Dead Pig Island Poetry Festival

"Born on the Scaffold"

Oblique line flattened by the wind...
feeling thickness

Inventio democratio

Each convergent explains itself

Black Velvet
...like Velvet
Black Viking
boat
black plastic
Valfs
sucks light out of the sky?
Black Diamond

TIME

Mondriaan
Landscape
of lines...

Seeing surface
A building without Detail?

1953

Boy's Room
village
square
cow

Painting studio
donkey door
strips with steel
twist and shout tent
Asphalt
Futures

Heat pumps warm the floors-
foundations go down 12cm
Gentlemen's Room
This World of His
wide horizon
Winter
summer
20cm

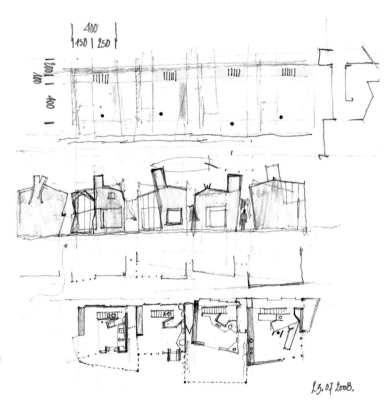

Jo Van Den Berghe,
't Raboes project, Eemnes,
Netherlands, 2013
The first sketch plan showing
the four houses that
eventually morphed into
the four workspaces of the
project.

23.07.2008.

trees and what the client described as a 'little wooden house'. Used to being patrons of architecture, the family noticed in an exhibition in Brussels the model of a wooden house 'archetype' designed and made by Belgian architect Jo Van Den Berghe. A conversation began and, after some time had passed, architect and client set a square-plan 'little wooden house' on a bridge-timber substructure emerging from a pond that is also an inlet from the inland sea. Reached by a narrow bridge, its four sides fold down to make decks.

Here in this house the conversation shifted to the design of the main complex, and its role on the client's imagined civic spine. 'Obviously, as we are on a polder, we should make bricks on the site and build it out of these!' they said. 'That's of the place and it saves transport.' Jo was thinking about his grandmother's house and the brick chimney nearby. He was playing with arches and vaults and corbels. He drew parallel brick walls, and considered

Leon van Schaik, research
ideogram, 15 April 2014
Drawn at the conclusion of
researching the project.

how to roof them. Vaults? Tripods holding a steel beam and glass like an industrial conservatory? 'Too many technical issues – how do we power a kiln for the bricks?' the conversation concluded. 'Maybe rammed earth?' Jo drew these walls and worked on how to found and to cap them. Maybe a grass roof, rather than a glass roof?

'But it's about small boats,' they mused. 'And these are mostly wood.' They went to study a species of small boat in danger of extinction, and dreamed of making water transport work again. Jo detailed clapboard roofs and sidings, and ridge-cappings made of twin sheets of copper, cut in a 'punk' zigzag to discourage birds from roosting. The building became a monolith in wood, changes in direction picked out with precious metal. 'Too many details! Can't we do a building without detail?' the conversation burned itself out. 'Boats have sails!' the conversation reignited. They studied new materials for sails, visited factories, looked at prototypes of lightweight cars. Jo designed a steel frame, and systems of cables and pulleys that tensioned the sail skins over the frame, and also served to pull boats up the slipway. He designed heavy curtains rather than doors.

Meanwhile the brief was refined. There were not to be four dwellings, only the other components. In the design, four childlike house-with-chimney profiles morphed from the polder edge back to the moorings, twisting and distorting across the programme, 'tortured by the wind', adding mini gables for each new function and sheltering a 'village square'. Adding Picasso and

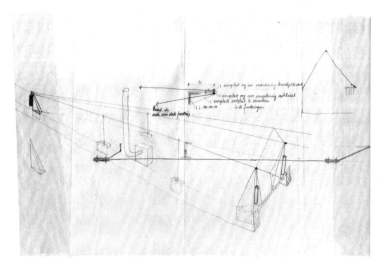

Jo Van Den Berghe,
't Raboes project, Eemnes,
Netherlands, 2013
Drawing of a sail-cloth
version of the project.

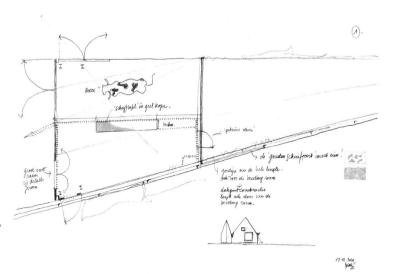

Jo Van Den Berghe,
't Raboes project, Eemnes,
Netherlands, 2013
Sketch plan showing a cow
in a byre alongside the
'gentleman's room'.

Jo Van Den Berghe,
't Raboes project, Eemnes,
Netherlands, 2013
Long elevation showing how
the building sucks in light as
if made from black velvet.

Braque Cubist thickness complicated the rational Piet Mondrian order of
the landscape. One of those functional additions was a cow byre in the
'gentleman's room', separated only by a glass wall.

This is the room in which the patron and his peers will meet, drink fine
whisky and smoke fine cigars while looking across the wide expansive surface

Jo Van Den Berghe,
't Raboes project, Eemnes,
Netherlands, 2013
The building seems to be
painted in space: the EPDM
fabric covers the door and
window frames so that the
glass and the matt black
doors read as being in the
same plane as the building
skin.

of the polder, the massing skies above, musing about future projects. 'But
the cow will stare at you through the glass wall! And maybe drop dung
at awkward moments!' 'Exactly!' Jo went on holiday to Norway in a black
mood. There he saw churches roofed with the black-tarred hulls of upturned
boats. He recalled seeing, on the farms surrounding the site, the black-plastic
tarpaulins used to wrap silage. 'EPDM!' he tossed into the conversation
(referring to ethylene propylene diene monomer, a type of synthetic rubber
used to make wetsuits). 'We already have the steel structure, now we fill that
with composite metal and insulation construction panels and anneal EPDM to
that. Self-cleaning in rain. No gutters, no down pipes, no details!'

The project took off. The foundation piles go down 20 metres (65 feet)
and they provide heat pumps warming all the slabs. The steel frame was
made and flawlessly assembled on site. Then it was fully closed in with the
panels, and holes were cut in for the high-specification metal window- and
doorframes. The EPDM was then rolled on, covering the entire building right
over the frames to glass and door edges, with any cut-off rectangles arced
into quarter circles to defy picking fingers. A polder sits below sea level.
As artists have observed for hundreds of years, light pools in these lands
with high horizons. And the black building soaks up light – sucking it out
of the sky, looking like black velvet. From nearby it seems a shadow on the
landscape; close up it has the mystery of a stage set, an unlikely and joyfully

Companion to 't Raboes
project: Clancy Moore,
Quarry House, near
Dublin, 2013
Built across the mouth
of a quarry in an area of
outstanding natural beauty,
this house has the qualities
of a stealth bomber, melting
away into the plantation
topography.

unsettling magic. As it has no details, it feels as if one has stepped into a painting in which the building is simply the colour black, the windows silvery black, the doors a muted nearly matt black.

These conversations took place over a period of six years. For the patron, they wound in and out of many entrepreneurial projects. For the architect who works 'inventio et executio',[5] with every design idea immediately being a construction idea, the conversations paralleled a research into the poetics of his particular spatial intelligence, finding its roots in his childhood memories of his grandmother's house, and working its way up from that realisation through all of his built projects and all of his dreams of making architecture. The conversations 'exhausted themselves', he says, as each design in turn surfaced his deep poetics of materials: the familiar clay, wood, glass and steel and then the new materials of the 21st century.

Jo Van Den Berghe, 't Raboes project, Eemnes, Netherlands, 2013
View of the 'boys' room' at the left, utility rooms in the centre and the boat shed to the right.

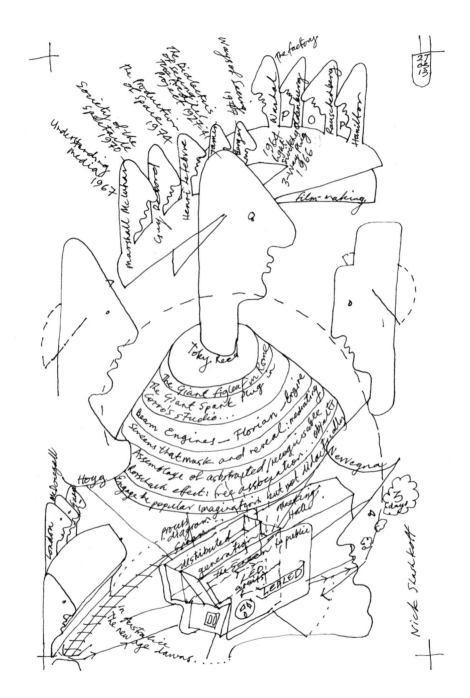

Understanding media 1967

Society of the Spectacle 1970

the Production of Space 1974

The Dialectics of Seeing (Arcades Project) 1974

Marshall McLuhan

Guy Debord

Henri Lefebvre

James Stirling "One-Stop shop"

1964 Warhol

Capt. Fantastic 3-Way play opening 1966

the factory

P O P

Rauschenberg

Hamilton

film-making.

Q

Toby Reed

The Giant figleaf in front
The Giant Spark plug
Corso's studio...
Beam Engines — Florian — engine
Screens that mask and reveal: mediating
Assemblage of abstracted/recognisable objects
Rorschach effect: free association... but not literally
engage the popular imagination

0

0

0

London McDougall

Hoyg

provocation

process
diagram
Green

distributed
generation
the factory
L.E.D
artist
LEDLED

In Australia
the new age dawns...

meeting
Hall

3 days

23

9

DD

44

Nick Stockett

Leon van Schaik, research
ideogram, 27 March 2013
Drawn at the conclusion of
researching the project.

Precinct Energy Project, Dandenong, Australia[6]

Peter Hogg + Toby Reed Architects (PHTR), 2013

At last in Australia, in Dandenong, as all over Europe, there is a district
developed around its own pocket power generator, converting natural gas to
electricity and pumping the resulting hot water to the surrounding buildings
where absorption chillers provide cooling when heating is not required.
Architects PHTR establish a poetics for this new paradigm.

Peter Hogg + Toby Reed
Architects, Precinct Energy
Project, Dandenong,
Australia, 2013
Facing the new pedestrian
route to the precinct.

What, then, does the new age finally dawning look like? Dandenong is
Melbourne's long-underprivileged central business district twin, being
rejuvenated by Places Victoria, a state development agency with in this
instance the vision to embrace the new. Seeking a location close to the core
of the redeveloped civic and commercial heart of the city, PHTR were asked
to establish whether the power station could be housed in a retained but
derelict Masonic hall. This proved to be an uneconomic proposition, and

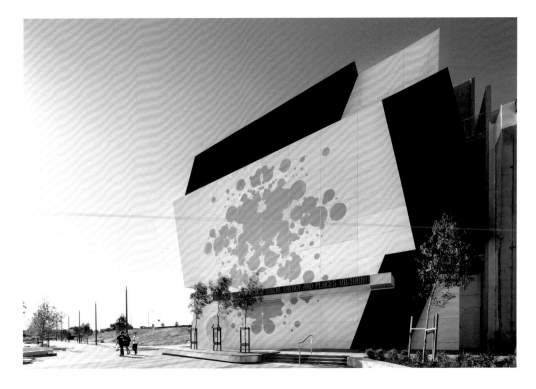

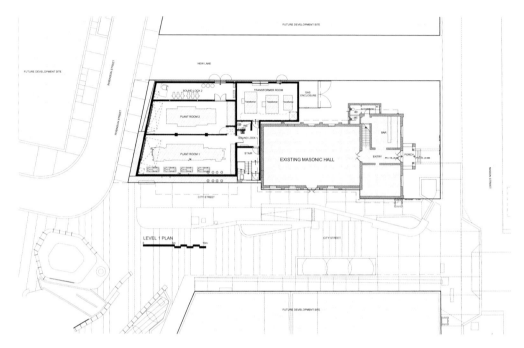

Inside the plan, labels read:

FUTURE DEVELOPMENT SITE

NEW LANE

FUTURE DEVELOPMENT SITE

ROBINSON STREET

SOUND LOCK 2

PLANT ROOM 2

PLANT ROOM 1

SOUND LOCK

STAIR

TRANSFORMER ROOM

GAS ENCLOSURE

EXISTING MASONIC HALL

BAR

ENTRY

PORCH

MASON STREET

CITY STREET

LEVEL 1 PLAN

CITY STREET

FUTURE DEVELOPMENT SITE

the architects, expertly shepherded by the client, Nick Shashkoff of Places Victoria, were given three days to develop a design for the cleared site immediately behind the Masonic hall. The new site, on the corner of the recently landscaped Station North Plaza and the City Street Mall leading to the new municipal centre, is in a direct line of sight from the railway station. It is a pivot to the public space of the new city. The facade of the old Masonic hall has the public face that classicism so readily affords, but it faces away.

The architects were asked to celebrate the civic importance of this position, and also to communicate to the passing public the excitement of this new form of power generation. How long did the design take? Three days. The principles of the design were already known: two rectangular engine rooms at the lower level, with a removable wall to allow the engines to be installed in two stages, and to be removed for servicing; an upper level for boilers; another upper level housing radiators to reject heat that is not utilised by the precinct heating system; banks of air intakes; acoustic attenuating devices – concrete walls, massive thermal and sound insulation; control rooms. So the programme requirements of two stacked rectangles with manifolds of ducting at one end and vertically articulated piping fell readily into place.

Peter Hogg + Toby Reed Architects, Precinct Energy Project, Dandenong, Australia, 2013
Plan showing the relationship to the existing Masonic hall, and indicating in dark tone the machinery that the building houses.

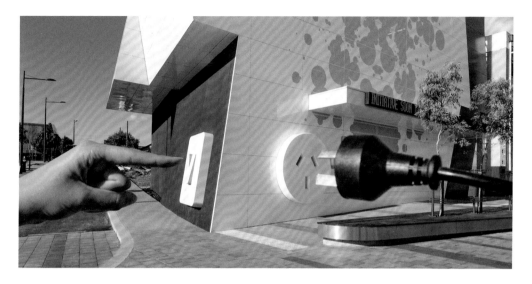

Peter Hogg + Toby Reed Architects, Precinct Energy Project, Dandenong, Australia, 2013
View showing artificial-turf-clad opening walls and giant switch.

The civic and didactic design took longer to prepare. Around fifty years of thinking supports the design. Walter Benjamin (*The Arcades Project*, 1927–40), Marshall McLuhan (*Understanding Media*, 1964) and Guy Debord (*Society of the Spectacle*, 1967), among others, have been haunting the imagination of Toby Reed (principal at PHTR), whose filmmaking gives him profound insight into how these thinkers have observed and theorised the changing relations between us and space. The artists who worked their way through these changes also haunt Toby: Andy Warhol and his lively New York studio The Factory; Claes Oldenburg and his sculptures of utilitarian household objects (electrical plugs, cutlery) enlarged to a massive scale; Robert Rauschenberg incorporating found popular objects into assemblages; and Richard Hamilton ennobling everyday domestic objects such as a pop-up toaster – these all dwell in Toby's imagination.

Peter Hogg + Toby Reed Architects, Precinct Energy Project, Dandenong, Australia, 2013
Elevation to the narrow street at the rear of the plant, showing the relationship to the existing Masonic hall and the diagram that uses engineering symbols to describe the process housed by the building.

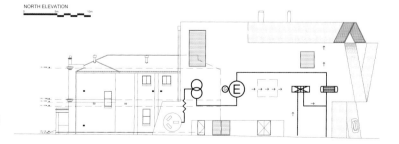

Rather as the Masonic hall has a classical face, Toby faced the long sides of the engine house with perforated screens, one to be read from the railway station, the other facing what will eventually be a narrow street. The forward screen presents a 'free association' of abstracted but recognisable elements. Through more transparent bubbles, elbows of pipework can be seen. And running along this face is an LED-messaging canopy. Here too, on the left-hand corner as you approach from the station, there is a large, human-scale socket outlet sculpture. Just around the corner beyond this, on the angled artificial-turf demountable wall of engine room two, is a giant double switch sculpture. These are both enamelled aluminium. The rear screen uses engineering symbols to diagram the processes at work inside, a diagram culminating in a second oversize socket on the diagonally opposite corner of engine room one.

Peter Hogg + Toby Reed Architects, Precinct Energy Project, Dandenong, Australia, 2013
View of the elevation to the narrow street as built.

The two boiler houses sit alongside each other, but one is canted forward, the other backward, as if to suggest that they might work against each other on a crank shaft. Inside there is a palpable excitement that comes from seeing a process in its entirety. The currently installed engine has the scale of

Peter Hogg + Toby Reed Architects, Precinct Energy Project, Dandenong, Australia, 2013
View of the first boiler to be installed.

a steam engine. It has a persona, a quality that giant plants have lost as we regard them as abstract 'infrastructure'. The minder of the plant, an engineer, talks of them with the sort of affection we remember from the *Thomas the Tank Engine* children's books and television series. The feeder ducts are lined with beautifully crafted columns of attenuators, making miniature but massive architectures, and these thrill the architect as much as the expanses of aluminium foil make him think of Warhol's Factory.

The architects have created a design that is in conversation with the engineering poetics of the interior functions and of a public expression of those functions, drawing on thoroughly researched lineages for both aspects of the design.

Companion to Precinct Energy Project: Konstantin Melnikov, Narkomtiazhprom, concept for Red Square, Moscow, 1934
In the foreground is a giant ball bearing framing a pair of axe-headed towers. The proposal symbolised the advance of industrialisation.

Arrow Studio, Tylden, Victoria, Australia[7]

Peter Hogg + Toby Reed Architects (PHTR), 2013

Not understanding that its own knowledge base arises from our spatial intelligence, architecture has largely failed to make society aware of the benefits of spatial thinking. The capacity of practical poetics to capture our aspirations is all too little known. Here is a project that most people could afford if they knew what architects can do.

The Arrow Studio has a poetics that is practical and witty, which situates itself in the history of the shed in architecture and expresses a family's intergenerational interest in art. How did this project come about? A family grew up in Melbourne; the parents had interests in the arts, the mother painted, some of the children painted. The children made friends with – among others – architects Peter Hogg and Toby Reed. Time passed and the father, widowed and living on a wooded block in a small village in central Victoria, sought to remember his wife and the love of painting she had engendered. The idea sparked a suggestion from his children that he ask their architect friends to create something appropriate, albeit with a very modest budget – marginally more than would purchase and insulate an off-the-peg shed.

Peter Hogg + Toby Reed Architects, The Arrow Studio, Tylden, Victoria, Australia, 2013
The gallery at dusk sits on the lawn as if it had been parked there and may move off at any moment.

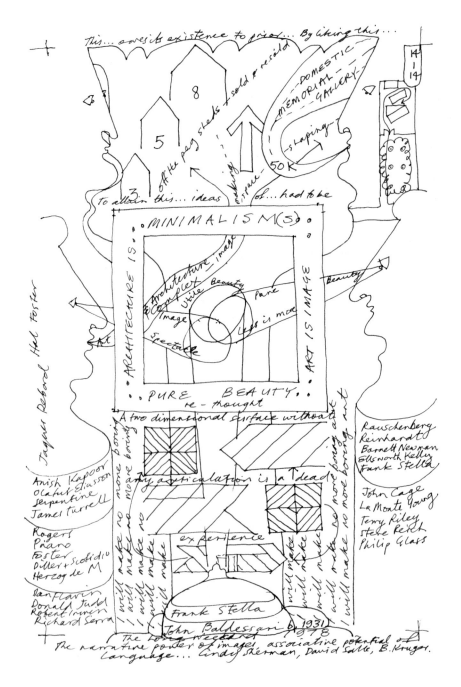

This... owes its existence to prior... By liking this...

DOMESTIC – MEMORIAL – GALLERY

8

5

– sloping –

off the peg steals sold & resold

3

To attain this... ideas ...making... space... of... had to be

– 50 K

MINIMALISM(S)

ARCHITECTURE IS

Architecture image

Complet Beauty

uive Beauty

Image

Pure

Less is more

Spectacle

Beauty

ART IS IMAGE

PURE — BEAUTY
re-thought

A two dimensional surface without

Jaques Debord Hal Foster

Anish Kapoor
Olafur Eliasson
Serpentine
James Turrell

Rogers
Piano
Foster + Scofidio
Diller + de M
Herzog de M

Dan Flavin
Donald Judd
Robert Irwin
Richard Serra

any articulation is a 'dead

I will make no more boring
I will make no more boring
I will make no
I will make

will make no more boring art
will make no more boring art
will make no more boring art
will make no more boring art
I will make no more boring art

experience

Rauschenberg
Reinhardt
Barnett Newman
Ellsworth Kelly
Frank Stella

John Cage
La Monte Young
Terry Riley
Steve Reich
Philip Glass

Frank Stella

John Baldessari b. 1931
The Long Weekend 1978
The narrative power of images, associative potential of
language... Cindy Sherman, David Salle, B. Kruger.

At the time of the commission, Toby Reed and his partners in practice were already engaged in designing and building a series of passive climate-modifying houses using new German technology. To meet the target budget for this 4-by-8-metre (13-by-26-foot) design, some deft manoeuvres were needed, separating the design and construction processes but linking both to this new technology. The builder, who was adept at using this technology, was pre-selected. Off-site and in the advanced technology context, the design was finalised. Plywood has been used structurally, and the highly insulated walls and roof are sheathed in galvanised sheeting lapped diagonally. Venetian-style narrow vertical windows puncture the end walls where they meet the side walls, flooding these picture-carrying planes with light.[8]

Timber battens provide shading and screening at each end, convexly to the east and concavely to the west. A south-facing clerestory window in

Peter Hogg + Toby Reed Architects, The Arrow Studio, Tylden, Victoria, Australia, 2013
Slot windows and a clerestory strip on the shaded elevation flood the gallery walls with light.

Peter Hogg + Toby Reed Architects, The Arrow Studio, Tylden, Victoria, Australia, 2013
The site plan shows how the house is set at an angle to the north–south rectangle of the plot; the gallery to the north takes a mediating angle between the house and the garden shed.

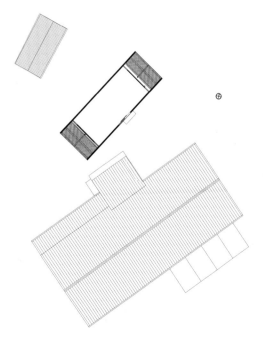

Leon van Schaik, research ideogram, 14 January 2014
Drawn at the conclusion of researching the project.

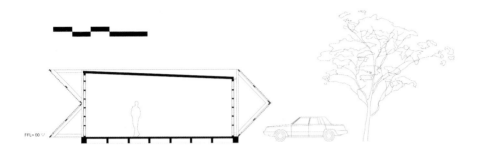

polycarbonate, with the entry door below, completes the ensemble. The gallery is sited at a slight angle to the house, and beyond it there is indeed a bought shed.

So much for the pragmatics. What has been provided is a shimmering architectural wonder, an object – as the architects intended – of 'pure beauty' that captures the imagination with its suggestion of being a motorhome, casually parked, evoking thoughts of journeys completed and of those to come. From some angles, it seems almost monumental in scale, and at night it effervesces like a recently landed spaceship. Inside, pictures hang on the walls in the process of being curated, old chairs make it homely, and it is always coolly comfortable.

Happenstance? Not at all. Toby, versed in art and filmmaking as well as in his own discipline, was completely aware and calculating in designing this

Peter Hogg + Toby Reed Architects, The Arrow Studio, Tylden, Victoria, Australia, 2013
Elevation showing the cladding pattern, and section showing the concave and convex end screens.

Peter Hogg + Toby Reed Architects, The Arrow Studio, Tylden, Victoria, Australia, 2013
At sunset, the Arrow glows with light as if it were preparing to lift off into the night.

Peter Hogg + Toby Reed
Architects, The Arrow
Studio, Tylden, Victoria,
Australia, 2013
In the afternoon, the gallery
seems about to float off into
the Australian bush, subject
of the paintings that it will
house.

tiny gallery. A constructed north-point arrow, the building hovers between
being an 'image' – that anathema of 1960s minimalism – and being
an industrial object of simply utilitarian beauty, eschewing reference to
anything other than itself. And yet, the square elevations of the convex and
concave ends are divided and barred up diagonally but in reverse to each
other, one forming a diamond motif, the other that of an 'X'. Signification,
this architect knows, is inescapable. The valency of the Arrow in its form
and in its about-to-depart siting, in its naming, in its glimmering in sunlight
and in its glowing in artificial light, is a calculated scenographic construct
arising from a lifetime spent in and around film. Toby Reed's father Colin
Eggleston directed *Long Weekend* (1978), an environmental horror film
about our relationship with nature and the bush, while Toby most notably
made a 2013 documentary on Peter Corrigan, the Melbourne architect
whose use of imagery mystifies and annoys Europeans.[9] The Arrow is
unusually elusive as an object in space. Each facade reads autonomously as
a two-dimensional graphic, yet as you walk around the building it seems to
twitch into three dimensions at each oblique, flickering between the two
graphics in view. This is a moment reminiscent of the filmmaking of Sergei
Eisenstein (1898–1948), a 'montage of attractors' enjoined to create a vision
in the mind of the viewer,[10] a vision that is – as the photographs attest –
uncanny and otherworldly, even monumental.

And to be sure, Toby is thoroughly conscious of the arguments within which
he is designing. He discusses Hal Foster's 2011 book, *The Art–Architecture*

Complex, a discourse that excoriates the late capitalist appropriation of the image into an 'architecture of the spectacle', or an architecture of 'the ancient Roman *panem et circenses* [bread and circuses], only without the bread', as critic Rowan Moore has put it.[11] While designing, Toby considered the pursuit of pure beauty by minimalists in art and in architecture, and was mindful of the critique that claws back a position for architecture as the utile art. He knows that this shed has to be in the lineage of the Sydney architect Philip Cox's romance with 19th-century wool-shearing sheds and with luxury houses in the manner of these now romantic ruins.[12] He knows that Lacaton & Vassal's Latapie House (1993) at Floirac in France lurks on the mental horizon. In a sense, in the Arrow, he paraphrases the conceptual artist John Baldessari's word work *Painting for Kubler* (2010): 'This [structure] owes its existence to prior [structures of its kind]. By liking this solution, you should not be blocked in your continued acceptance of prior [versions]. To attain this [design], ideas of [the shed] had to be rethought.'[13] He further aligns himself with two other Baldessari works: 'A two-dimensional surface without any articulation is a dead experience' – the Arrow is alive; 'I will not make any more boring art' – the Arrow is not minimalist, nor is it imagist; it hovers tellingly between these zones, it is pure magic.[14] And it could be in your backyard.

Companion to the Arrow Studio: Amanda Levete Architects, new courtyard and entry to the Victoria and Albert Museum, London, due for completion in 2016
The design of the courtyard inverts the object-to-field relationships exploited in the Arrow Studio, and an internal scalar ambiguity results.

Borgarfjördur College, Borgarnes, Iceland

Kurtogpi Architects, 2008

Crisis is almost synonymous with Iceland: volcanic and financial. The culture has been nurtured through centuries of survival in the far north, with an extreme agricultural cycle in which what grew in the summer, flora and fauna, had to be harvested and preserved. Seed stock was locked away for the next growing season. Surrounding this was the immensely hard practice of fishing. This dominating duality forged intense creative practice and an instinct for individuality. Through these qualities Iceland has shrugged off crisis and become a wealthy country. The career of architect Steinþór Kári Kárason exposes the poetics of this battle between crisis and individuality.

Icelandic architect Steinþór Kári Kárason and his partner Ásmundur Hrafn Sturluson, in the practice Kurtogpi Architects, attended the opening of Borgarfjördur College, a secondary school founded and owned by the local community, in 2008, ten days after everyone became aware that there was a global financial crisis. This was the largest project that the practice had undertaken up to that date, and subsequent projects have been much smaller.

The school commission came through a director of a nearby business college who liked the work of the firm, and who came from Borgarnes, a town 75 kilometres (47 miles) north of Reykjavik and equally south of the next centre with a secondary college. The business college, along with an agricultural university in the area, was a driving force in the local campaign to build a school, and all the major local businesses pledged financial support for the project. A design committee was established, as was a school organisation design committee. Both were working from scratch, and both were innovating rather than replicating existing models.

Kurtogpi Architects, Borgarfjördur College, Borgarnes, Iceland, 2008
View of the College and Aula from the entry side.

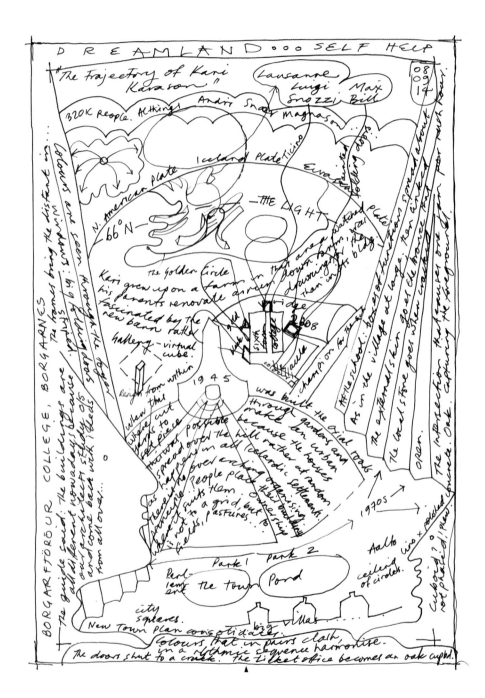

"The Trajectory of Kari Karason"

320K People. Althingi

Lausanne, Luigi Snozzi, Max Bill

08 09 14

Andri Snær Magnason

N. American plate

Iceland Plate tectonic

Eva plante

telling days

— THE LIGHT —

66° N

the golden Circle

Kari grew up on a farm
his parents renovate ancient down farm
fascinated by the
new barn rather
gallery — virtual cube.

A file school

As in the village

The local store goes when washed

The diplomatics

1945

was built the axial road
through gardens and
make the urban
because the houses
spread over the hill rather at random
as happens in all Icelandic settlement
people place their building
where it suits them. Ownership
is not to a grid, but to
fields, pastures.

1970s →

Aalto
ceiling of circles.

Park 1   Park 2

Parliament   The town   Pond

city squares.

New Town Plan consolidates   big villas

Colours that in pairs clash,
in a rhythmic sequence harmonise.
The doors shut to a crack. The ticket office becomes an oak cupboard.

Leon van Schaik, research ideogram, 8 September 2014
Drawn at the conclusion of researching the project.

The architects, who teach in the bachelor's-level architecture programme in Reykjavik and are fascinated by the ways in which Icelandic settlements grow, observed the almost random placing of buildings in Borgarnes. Sites are usually old fields with common-law boundaries. Buildings are placed on these at the whim of each owner, obeying priorities formed by these individuals. Even in the capital, the seemingly planned order of Reykjavik, with its fan of streets emanating from the Hallgrímskirkja (1945–86), a church on the highest hill, was created in the early 20th century by driving the streets through the areas of paddock left between the existing houses.

In the design of the school, the architects deployed the major programmatic elements of the school as two separate parts, nudging a rocky ridge and splayed apart by a space angled to the southwest between them, with a skirt of circulation and foyer space linking them at ground level. The college classrooms, in three blocks, form one part, and a hall (the Aula) intended to operate as an auditorium for the village as well as the school hall forms the other. This separation gives the hall the chance to function autonomously and with an atmosphere other than that of an assembly hall. The school facilities on two levels surround a wide corridor. Where this reaches an external wall there are windows, deeply inset with seats and surrounded mostly in black,

Kurtogpi Architects, Borgarfjördur College, Borgarnes, Iceland, 2008
Plan showing the ridge and the Aula to the left, the entry face to the top and the school block to the left.

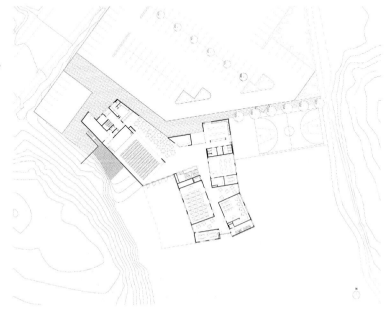

Kurtogpi Architects,
Borgarfjördur College,
Borgarnes, Iceland, 2008
A summer view.

with just one in honey-coloured oak. These act as huge picture frames, grabbing the mountains across the fjord and dragging them forward onto the picture plane, in a celebration of what for most of the year is inaccessible and remote. The building is clad in a brass that anodises to the colour of the rocks in the ridges nearby. The colour in the building comes from the striped painting of the folding doors that separate the hall from the foyer and circulation spaces. By artist Thor Vigfússon, these stripes completely remove any sense of there being a wall of doors, imposing a syncopated colour rhythm that can be seen through the glass wall of the northern entry front. Strong winds from the southwest made entry from that direction impossible.

The building is designed, it seems, for the long periods when it is experienced from inside, with only the views to the brightly lit coloured elements – the folding doors and the locker doors – giving an external invitation towards the outside.

The massive, boldly framed windows have the effect that ornate gilded frames have on paintings: the position of the observer is emphasised, while the picture plane itself segues between being the surface of the glass and being a far-distant prospect viewed through the window of a palace. At the college the effect in the winter is to frame interior activity as a painting through which ghostly traces of the snow-covered landscape can be seen, and in summer to bring the green flush of distant grass and moss slopes right up to the eye.

Steinþór and Ásmundur have a community of practice that embraces the artists and writers of Iceland, and this framing of inside and outside is no accident. In a small gallery in the city the architects have created a virtual white cube in a space penetrated by columns by putting a square of lights on the ceiling, a square that reads as the pure face of a cube with the floor-to-ceiling height as its ruling dimension. The illusion is further enhanced by lining out the side walls with technical and storage corridors so that their inner faces are perpendicular to the street face, while a rear wall conceals within the baggy remnant space an additional hanging space, picture storage racks, a director's office and a lounge library.

Kurtogpi Architects, Borgarfjördur College, Borgarnes, Iceland, 2008
The striking and unlikely colour combinations of artist Thor Vigfússon make the folding door surrounding two sides of the Aula, here seen from the courtyard, an always fresh experience.

Kurtogpi Architects,
Borgarfjördur College,
Borgarnes, Iceland, 2008
A stairwell, in the context
of the folding doors and the
foyer ceiling.

At the school, a kiosk at the entry doubles as a ticket office for the Aula and a bar, and when its oak shutters slide open it becomes a golden cube. Material use refers to primal matter, ageing – as the architects state – in a 'natural and beautiful way'. Floors are oak where people spend most time, polished concrete in circulation areas or – in stairways where acoustic dampening is a good idea – plain black linoleum. Areas where there is traffic have white-tiled walls, the grout omitted to give an acoustic absorbency and visual sharpness. Surrounded by such a massive and rocky landscape, adding skins of plaster to surfaces seems very artificial, and this the architects avoid. Handrails are strap metal, sinuously crafted. Some of the ceilings are exposed services masked by metal mesh or plaster cratered with varying sizes of circular holes, some of which house sprinklers; the fire brigade had to be convinced that sprinklers worked in these situations. Lights are circles of fluorescents behind the mesh. These circles were intended to manifest in the hard landscape as rings of grass, but that has yet to happen.

Doors have specially rebated stiles and close flush with their broad architraves. The door furniture is tubular in form, as are the bathroom fittings.

But this is not catalogue design. Everything has been drawn. Writing about the Icelandic sagas, Gwyn Jones states that these were very much crafted through writing during the long winters, on vellum that was in abundant supply given the cull-and-survive agricultural cycle of early settlement.[15] Rather than being the remembered and recorded remnants of an aural tradition, the sagas were developed in written form. Steinþór grew up on a farm in the interior, as his parents renovated its dilapidated buildings. A new barn was built. What captured Steinþór's imagination was not the erection, portal by portal, but the drawings that the builders referred to. These were what he pored over during the long winters, and his architecture has that considered quality, crafted over long periods, worked and reworked, refined.

How fortunate for him that he studied under Luigi Snozzi, an architect from the canton of Ticino in southern Switzerland who used the town of Monte Carasso as a laboratory for an architecture of small projects with urban embraces spreading through the town and with forms that evolved from the place. It suited Steinþór's embedded Icelandic architectural passion exactly.

Kurtogpi Architects, Borgarfjördur College, Borgarnes, Iceland, 2008
General view of the school showing to the left the fold of rock that determines its one boundary and some of the randomly placed other elements of the town.

Iceland is a very large island, bigger than Ireland, but has only 320,000 residents. Everyone in a creative sphere knows everyone, and all know the sagas of the past and the writers of modern times. Bookshops stocked with books in Icelandic flourish. Steinþór admires the book *Dreamland: A Self-Help Manual for a Frightened Nation* (2006) by Andri Snær Magnason.[16] This

book exposes the ways in which politicians simplify issues, combining them into singular fictive crises that enable them to persuade people to support simplistic solutions that serve only the interests of the wealthy. For instance, population growth indicates that Iceland needs to generate 40,000 jobs over the coming decades. Crisis! Build giant thermal electricity plants and smelt aluminium! Any considered analysis shows, argues Magnason, that this produces a spike of jobs during construction, but very few ongoing jobs. Meanwhile vast areas of potential interest to sophisticated visitors (tourism, possibly of the lowest common denominator kind, has become the country's largest earner) are destroyed for the benefit of global companies with no interest in Icelanders' wellbeing. The book argues that investing the same amount of money in education without a preconceived end goal, and allowing people to develop their own future, is a better option.

Steinþór is evidence of this. The practice survived boom and bust, in both situations working with a wider community that knows and respects their deep architectural thinking. Magnason argues that every farm, given the right to craft and promote its own produce, would serve the same sophisticated local and international market. Icelandair has made Iceland a hub between North America and Europe, and as the Blue Lagoon shows, this can deliver unique experiences. As if to prove the point, the Borgarnes College hums with the excitement of young people finding themselves and their way. Investing in the young across Iceland, as it invested in Steinþór and Ásmundur by sending them to Lausanne and London, and not in smelters seems absolutely the right thing to do. Such an approach is also a paradigm for the kind of architecture this book supports: not mega projects but thoughtful, locally embedded, healing, feeding, capturing and homing architectures.

Companion to Borgarfjördur College: McGarry Ní Éanaigh Architects, Coláiste Ailigh, Letterkenny, County Donegal, Ireland, 2014
The colours of the school, blue outside and often bright yellow inside, seem to tie the building to the Atlantic weather system, matching glowering skies and ingesting rays of sunshine.

RMIT Design Hub, Melbourne

Sean Godsell Architects, 2012

The practice of Sean Godsell is internationally acclaimed. You would think it arose in a situation lush with positive affirmation, but its poetics is forged in an adversarial local clime. Such resistance attends most innovation; maybe it cannot be avoided – after all, pearls result from grit in the oyster.

Mental frames crowd in on Sean's seemingly straightforward architectural agenda. Those who claim him as 'one of us' fail to understand the full significance of a poetics forged in adversity. No part of a Godsell building has not been mentally wrestled into being. Nothing is happenstance. There is no room in his process for a lucky accident post-rationalised into respectability. What are these frames? Many can be described, and each is not unique in its nature, but the concatenation of so many frames makes for a very particular practice, even on the universal stage of architecture. The first frame is probably the first frame for every one of us.[17] Sean's father was an architect with modernist ambitions. Inspired by Frank Lloyd Wright, David Godsell designed a house for his family. It embodied every architectural understanding that he had established. It hugged its sloping, sandy site. It compressed space and then released it into a soaring top-lit volume. It located the kitchen so that his wife could observe the doings of her children as she went about her day. There was a studio where he worked. His son absorbed this vision.

'Who Architects Design For, and Who They Are When They Design' is the subtitle of an analysis of practice in the state of Victoria in Australia.[18] Architects design for their clients, yes, but as much as that they design for the approbation of their mentors and their peers. Who those are determines the way they frame their designing. Sean studied architecture at a school with a great history programme but an approach to design that he rebelled against. In a post-colonial Australian trajectory, Sean infused that British modernist context with a fascination for Sino-Japanese architecture, struck by the corridor-free, sliding-screen-divided plans and volumes of the Katsura Imperial Villa in Kyoto. Then he did his antipodean version of the 'Grand Tour', working in London for Sir Denys Lasdun. He also developed his admiration for the works of Le Corbusier, Kazuo Shinohara, Tadao Ando and others. Back home he worked for various practices, notably completing the Northern Melbourne Institute of Technical and Further Education campus

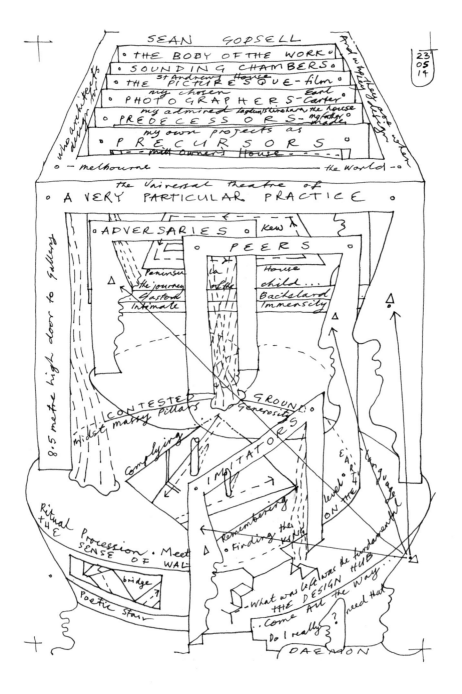

SEAN GODSELL

- THE BODY OF THE WORK
- SOUNDING CHAMBERS
- THE PICTURESQUE - film
- PHOTOGRAPHERS
- my admired
- PREDECESSORS
- my own projects as
- PRECURSORS
- mill owner's House

o — melbourne —————————————— the World --

the Universal Theatre of
○ A VERY PARTICULAR PRACTICE ○

○ ADVERSARIES ○ Kew
PEERS
House
child...
Backeland
Immensity

CONTESTED GROUND
Generosity
IMITATORS
language
ON the

Ritual Procession · Meet
SENSE OF WALL
bridge
Poetic Stair

what was left was the fundamental
THE DESIGN HUB
Come ALL the way...
Do I really need that?

DAEMON

Leon van Schaik, research ideogram, 23 May 2014
Drawn at the conclusion of researching the project.

Sean Godsell Architects, RMIT Design Hub, Melbourne, 2012
This image of the building plays up its iconic idealist form, while its humanist conception is concealed.

with Hassell Architects. Slowly he developed his own practice designing houses. On a steep and therefore affordable site in the Melbourne suburb of Kew, Sean created his own house, a floating box with a circulation path around its interior perimeter. This Sean acknowledges in Bachelardian terms as 'the journey of the child', a journey that concludes in the life of the adult.[19]

Known as the Kew House (1997), the building perches on the site and has a single open space along its north (sun-facing) flank and a series of bedroom and bathroom cells closed off by sliding doors along its southern flank.[20] At the eastern end there is a full-width wall of kitchen and services, and a long table stretches almost the full length. The western end projects out above street level and aims at the city centre skyline. Sean might as well have been pointing a bazooka, given the stunned reaction of his peers.

To understand Sean's poetics, consider the threshold to the Design Hub at RMIT: a level struck from the top corner of the site that runs downhill while accommodating a flush entrance and a compliant slope using triangulated bluestone paving.

Godsell recognises that photographs 'speak the designs back' to the designer, as do the sounding-board recognitions of his critics. These are crucial symbiotic relationships. Architects need photographers who understand their work, thinkers who can say, as does Hayley Franklin, his long-term colleague in the office: 'Yes! I recognise what you are doing!' Or: 'No! you've done that better before …'

Here are a few moments in the Design Hub that reveal the architect thinking. Sean has drawn in pencil every detail of the building. He drew his way around

Sean Godsell Architects, RMIT Design Hub, Melbourne, 2012
The subtle accommodation of the entry threshold to the slope to the left is achieved with triangulated pavers.

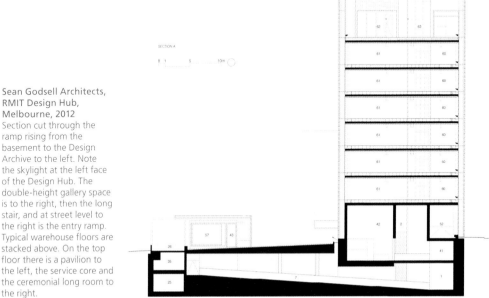

SECTION A

0 1   5   10m

Sean Godsell Architects, RMIT Design Hub, Melbourne, 2012
Section cut through the ramp rising from the basement to the Design Archive to the left. Note the skylight at the left face of the Design Hub. The double-height gallery space is to the right, then the long stair, and at street level to the right is the entry ramp. Typical warehouse floors are stacked above. On the top floor there is a pavilion to the left, the service core and the ceremonial long room to the right.

that difficult corner of the Design Hub, striking a level at which the circular glazed screen would terminate and sweep around from the south face along the western face and tie in with the soffit to the café a storey below. The entry parade seems to match the slope of the street – a carefully made illusion, because what is allowed as a pavement does not comply with regulations inside. Immediately after entering, there is a mesh in the floor leading your eye to a slit window that gives a glimpse to the gallery one floor below.

As you process up the internal ramp, passing the lifts and an entry to toilets, you rise up in parallel to the city's civic spine, reach another entry, turn, and walk back down alongside the white pews of a raked lecture hall exposed to public view via a glass partition wall. As you continue to descend past a service area entrance, you look onwards to a window out to the street to the south, and then down a long flight of stairs and landings to the basement level three floors below. The fundamental parti of the building through its several warehouse floors above and in its ritual spaces below is now inscribed on your mind.

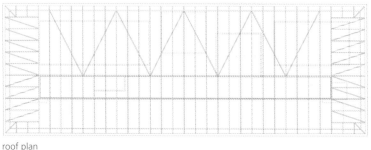

roof plan

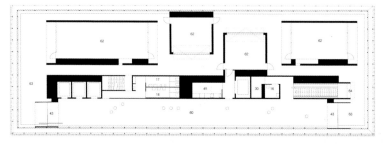

levels 7

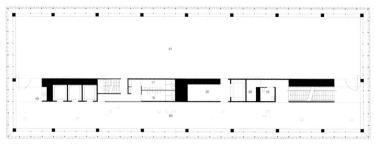

levels 2-6

This view is far from austere, and this differentiates Sean's poetics from all
his imitators and from his Japanese mentors. The interior walls and ceilings
are galvanised web mesh, a flecked and imprecise gridding that gives the
impression of fabric. As you float down the long stairs, another mesh insert
in the floor makes a noise at your feet and alerts you to a wider slot to the
gallery. Then there is a landing and an 8.5-metre- (28-foot-) high sliding
opening – not intended for normal entry – followed by a further descent.
At the end of this vista figures move past, some at ground level, some up
a ramp to the right and some in the street beyond. And when you arrive,
turning right, you enter a double-volume space centred on two columns,

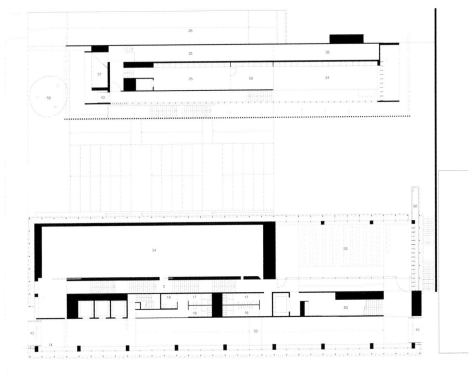

Ground Floor

antechamber to the biggest lecture space in the building. Light pours in down the face of the warehouse slab through a skylight. The ramp continues to slide on and up, and holding the hall in place there is an external version of the stair that you have descended. The forms are simple, all is orthogonal, yet you inhabit a picturesque interior.

There is one more frame to be described. On Sean's shoulder sits a daemon always asking: 'Do I really need that?' Abstracting goes on until what is left is 'the fundamental language' of the project. On the Swanston Street face this is powerfully revealed. A literal purist, that which Sean is not, would have carved out the ground to give the illusion that the sun-tracking disks of the external screen ran their course uninterrupted below street level. However, this building is not an ideal Miesian object compromised by its sloping site. It is a picturesque construct, and the snipping off of the skirt of the glazed skin along the pavement reveals the pragmatic poetics of this architecture. Compare this to the radiator bent to fit the overriding logic of Ludwig Wittgenstein's design for his sister's house (1928).

At this moment, in strong counterpoint to the iconic projections of photographers, the pragmatic humanism of Sean's approach becomes clear.[21]

Nonetheless this building is a critique of all around it. Standing at the base of the external courtyard, you look out between the slab of the Design Hub

Sean Godsell Architects, RMIT Design Hub, Melbourne, 2012
The Design Hub creates a critique of the less considered buildings around it.

and the pavilion of the Design Archive and you see a cacophony of mediocrity (John James Clark's City Baths (1904) and Lyons' Swanston Academic Building (2012) are not visible). You are moved to pity for the citizens who must inhabit a city so polluted by unambitious designing.

Ludwig Wittgenstein and Paul Engelmann, Haus Wittgenstein or Stonborough House, Kundmanngasse, Vienna, 1928
Wittgenstein focused on the windows, doors, doorknobs and radiators. This radiator was specially made to fit its axially correct position in the room.

Sean Godsell Architects, RMIT Design Hub, Melbourne, 2012
The discs on the east facade are cut to the slope of the pavement.

Companion to the RMIT Design Hub: Lina Bo Bardi, SESC Pompéia, São Paulo, early 1980s
A social and cultural centre built to defy demolition by right-wing elites.

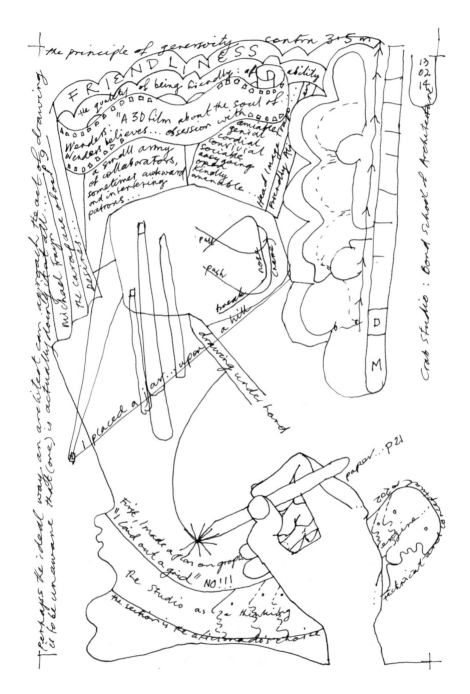

the principle of generosity   contra 3·5 m

FRIENDLINESS

the quality of being friendly : affability

"A 3D film about the soul of
Wenders believes... obsession with
amiable
a small army
genial
cordial
of collaborators,
convivial
sometimes awkward
sociable
and interfering
easy going
patrons.
open
kindly
amenable

(Head/Image Papa)

friendly fire

pull
push
break
a bit
rotate (Creme)

I placed a j apart... upward

drawing under hand

first : "made a plan on graph
"I laid out a grid"   NO!!!

the studio as "2i" thinking

the section is the sectional architect's choir

paper... p 21

2o go architectural
lot's
magazine
... technical

Perhaps the ideal way an architect can engage with the act of drawing is to be unaware that (one) is actually doing it at all.

Michael Fagan — p. 9

the caves are a record.

Crab Studio : Bond School of Architecture

13
03
14

Abedian School of Architecture, Robina, Queensland, Australia

CRAB studio (Cook Robotham Architectural Bureau), 2014

Many remark – as does critic Michael Frayn – that our buildings are 'the carapace of our desires'. Filmmaker Wim Wenders has embarked on 'a 3D project about the soul of buildings'. Few buildings express desires wittingly, their souls are suppressed by pragmatics, but CRAB studio projects have a smilingly practical poetics.

Of the architectures that are conscious, some marshal a rigorous ordering system and instruct us on how to use them. Gottfried Semper's neoclassical Polytechnikum in Zurich (1865) uses axial planning and a nested hierarchy of junctions and diminishing scales of rooms to ensure that we always know where we are relative to the central spine, and always know what degree of intimacy is appropriate in any space. This tradition continues. Once I worked for a disciple of Ludwig Mies van der Rohe as he designed an office complex for a factory. Day after day we drew different-sized grids on yellow butter paper, and he tested these against the programme: port cochère, entrance area, reception area, board room, offices for executives, an engineering studio, washrooms, tea kitchens, refuse area. Day after day he rejected the grids and asked for more. One day we arrived and he was drawing an elevation using Mies's steel detailing. Solved! We had the impression that to fit the ordering of the building, the occupants would wear business uniforms, buttoned-down collars and ties, pencil skirts and blouses. Blue shirts for the engineers, white shirts for the accountants.

Peter Cook's buildings are friendly. This is a slightly startling realisation in an architectural context. He and Colin Fournier called the Graz Kunsthaus (2003) 'the friendly alien'. That building does have the air of a shambling monster, an aspect most of us put down to resonances with drawings of an ambulant city from the avant-garde group Archigram, of which Peter was a co-founder in the 1960s. But the friendliness persists. The Abedian Architecture School at Bond University, carried out with Gavin Robotham, has a soul that is affable, amiable, genial, cordial, easy-going, open, kindly, amenable – and consciously so. And it is defiant in its desire for these qualities.[22] As Wenders notes, filmmakers and architects have much in common: both need numerous collaborators to realise their visions, and both have to deal with sometimes difficult patrons.[23]

Leon van Schaik, research ideogram, 13 February 2014
Drawn at the conclusion of researching the project.

Where do we look for the engines of the specific friendliness of this school of architecture? Firstly we know that there is a powerful vision informing the design. Peter Cook is a great educator and advocates a particular, experimental studio approach. He has run studios and critiqued studios almost everywhere. As he remarks (I paraphrase): 'I have a pretty good idea about what it takes to make a good school of architecture. Strangely, that has very little to do with the building that it might be in, so much depends on the educational vision and who is there on the ground. But if a building can help, I know how it can help!'[24]

And at Bond we have that vision: affable but determined. The amiability of the building is created by its ample and flowing volumes, while its instructive impulses are contained in the differentiated granulation of its cross sections, its topography-hugging, long section and its simple, programmatically direct plan. An internal street runs up the hill away from the entrance portico. Four huge scallops of concrete define one edge, a wall of cellular rooms the other. A floor plane is allowed to cascade back down from the rear, eddying around the scallops and so forming many different pools for studio groups.

CRAB studio, Abedian School of Architecture, Robina, Queensland, Australia, 2014
The Studio edge wall, with the entrance to the right.

High above and reached by stairs on the outer skins of the scallops is a mezzanine studio that overlooks the street and the double-volume lobe of space off the entrance to the ramp, a space that doubles up as exhibition and lecture space. Huge concrete mushroom plates with timber soffits roof over, supported by clusters of organically arranged columns.

Possibly their organic arrangement is a memory of the forest trees that they displace. The long overlooking corridors that run along the cellular side of the street lead to a 'nose' that juts out under the biggest of the mushroom plates. This houses the office of a head of school and a long thin faculty meeting room.

Some of the cells down the strip are configured for research teams, and all are for quieter work. The studios on the slope and the mezzanine are clipped between the undulating outer wall and the vertical bulges of the scallops, a pinching that gives just so much privacy, and encourages overlooking. And the hollows of the scallops cup crit spaces. The building bespeaks a specific educational model, conversationally and not dogmatically. This is a cathedral of learning; it could, says Peter, be used for 'recitals of Baroque music'.[25]

CRAB studio, Abedian School of Architecture, Robina, Queensland, Australia, 2014
Plans of the ground floor, level one and level two. The studios are at the lower edge, and the street runs between these and the other functions, with the directorial 'nose' at upper right.

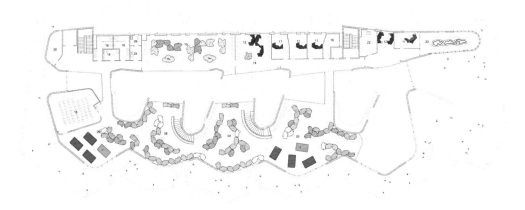

01: Street/ Linear Gallery
02: 'Crit' space within Scoop
03/04: Masters Studio 1
05: Foundation Masters Studio
06/07: Undergraduate Studio 1
08/09: Undergraduate Studio 2
10: Post Grad Space
11: Closed Office

12: Open Plan Office
13: Meeting Room
14: Staff Withdrawal
15: 'Black Box' Lecture Space
16: Department Storage
17: Furniture Storage
18: Toilet
19: Faculty Cafe/ Bar

20: Atelier
21: Meeting Room
22: Reception Suite Kitchen
23: Reception Suite
24: Student Tea/ Coffee Point
25: Forum
26: Student Resource Room
27: Staff Resource Room

28: Reading Room
29: Utility Room
30: Environmental Sciences Labs
31: Plant Room
32: Entrance Ramp
33: External Concrete Hardstand

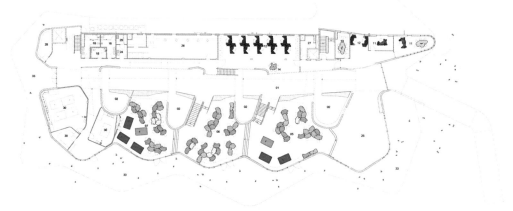

01: Street/ Linear Gallery
02: 'Crit' space within Scoop
03/04: Masters Studio 1
05: Foundation Masters Studio
06/07: Undergraduate Studio 1
08/09: Undergraduate Studio 2
10: Post Grad Space
11: Closed Office

12: Open Plan Office
13: Meeting Room
14: Staff Withdrawal
15: 'Black Box' Lecture Space
16: Department Storage
17: Furniture Storage
18: Toilet
19: Faculty Cafe/ Bar

20: Atelier
21: Meeting Room
22: Reception Suite Kitchen
23: Reception Suite
24: Student Tea/ Coffee Point
25: Forum
26: Student Resource Room
27: Staff Resource Room

28: Reading Room
29: Utility Room
30: Environmental Sciences Labs
31: Plant Room
32: Entrance Ramp
33: External Concrete Hardstand

1m   5m   10m

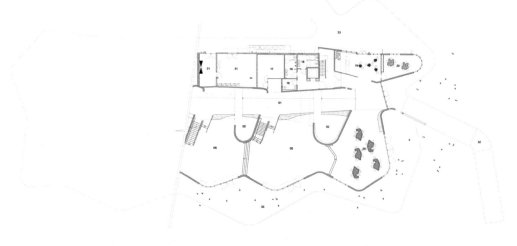

01: Street/ Linear Gallery
02: 'Crit' space within Scoop
03/04: Masters Studio 1
05: Foundation Masters Studio
06/07: Undergraduate Studio 1
08/09: Undergraduate Studio 2
10: Post Grad Space
11: Closed Office

12: Open Plan Office
13: Meeting Room
14: Staff Withdrawal
15: 'Black Box' Lecture Space
16: Department Storage
17: Furniture Storage
18: Toilet
19: Faculty Cafe/ Bar

20: Atelier
21: Meeting Room
22: Reception Suite Kitchen
23: Reception Suite
24: Student Tea/ Coffee Point
25: Forum
26: Student Resource Room
27: Staff Resource Room

28: Reading Room
29: Utility Room
30: Environmental Sciences Labs
31: Plant Room
32: Entrance Ramp
33: External Concrete Hardstand

1m   5m   10m

CRAB studio, Abedian
School of Architecture,
Robina, Queensland,
Australia, 2014
Mushroom plate roofs swell
out to shelter the entry from
sun and tropical rainstorms.

The collaboration process for the development and realisation of the design
lies in the culture of drawing and the way in which drawing works in a design
studio. Describing the drawing of an early Archigram project, Peter writes:
'First I made a plan on graph paper'.[26] This is not however a Miesian grid. It
is a graphic layout aide. We should not look for an ideal grid in this building.
Rather, we should look over Peter's shoulder as he draws. We do this quietly.
He writes: 'Perhaps the ideal way an architect can approach the act of

CRAB studio, Abedian
School of Architecture,
Robina, Queensland,
Australia, 2014
The 'nose' projecting under
the entry mushroom roof.

CRAB studio, Abedian
School of Architecture,
Robina, Queensland,
Australia, 2014
Studios are furnished with
tables designed by CRAB
studio.

drawing is to be unaware that he is actually doing it at all.'[27] It is only when
the thinking mind is stilled that all of the architect's knowledge can flow onto
the paper through the act of drawing. Another great teacher – the landscape
architect and Adjunct Professor at RMIT, Cath Stutterheim – was wont to get
her young students to draw complex objects like a bicycle while reading them
gripping stories that distracted their conscious attention and allowed holistic
observation. When Peter used graph paper, the designing was pretty much

Companion to Abedian School of Architecture: Cassandra Fahey, Smith Great Aussie House, Black Rock, Melbourne, 2007
Few other architects have been as refreshingly playful as Cassandra. Here the pleated ceiling achieves some of the same light-heartedness that the over-sailing roof plates of the Abedian School of Architecture deliver.

over. He was presenting the idea. Working in the CRAB studio on a design, on this design, I have the impression that Peter was drawing 'underhand', using the pencil to look up into the spaces as he drew the plans that we look down upon. In looking up he draws also the eyes and minds of his collaborators into the space, so that they can work on particular aspects of the designing – the timber soffits perhaps, or the jigsaw joinery and furniture – while keeping in mind the whole section, that holder, as Peter writes, of 'the conceptual and the technical'.[28] Together Peter and his collaborators 'tweak and pull and push' the design into being.

Sounds easy. But there are dangers ahead for anyone who sets out to make a friendly building without the years of drawing, studio working, talking, thinking, assimilating. In the 1960s Richard Hamilton ran a foundation year in Fine Art at the University of Newcastle upon Tyne. It consisted of intense weekly modules, one of which concerned the difficulty posed by the innate human propensity to see a face or a head in any aggregation of marks and shapes. A smiling face does not a friendly building make; it causes the visual equivalent of an earworm. No building of Peter's does this, even though parts are anthropomorphically named. A conversation that loops through a consistent set of concerns on a more and more certain terrain underlies this work. There is a very English, unstated but determined, political claim at work here. Conscious thinking architecture is good for you and for all of us, and we should all have access to it.

CRAB studio, Abedian School of Architecture, Robina, Queensland, Australia, 2014
The internal street rising up the slope of the site, with crit spaces and studios to the right.

References

1. See Richard Dawkins, *The Selfish Gene* [1976, revised 2006], Folio Society (London), 2011, pp 193–206 and 207–38.
2. Simon Schama, 'Preface', in *The Embarrassment of Riches: An Interpretation of Dutch Culture in the Golden Age*, Vintage Books (New York), 1987, p xi.
3. See Daniel Kahneman, *Thinking, Fast and Slow*, Allen Lane (London), 2011.
4. Ingmar Bergman (dir), *Fanny and Alexander*, 1982.
5. See Jo Van Den Berghe, *Theatre of Operations, or: Construction Site as Architectural Design*, unpublished PhD thesis, RMIT, Melbourne, 2012.
6. A version of this account appeared in *Architectural Review Asia Pacific*, no 131, Spring 2013, pp 84–9.
7. A version of this account appeared in *Architecture Australia*, vol 103, no 2, March/April 2014, pp 34–8.
8. On windows in Venetian houses, see Steen Eiler Rasmussen, *Experiencing Architecture* [1959], The MIT Press (Cambridge, MA), 1964, p 206.
9. Toby Reed (dir), *The Architecture of Edmond and Corrigan*, commissioned by RMIT Gallery for the exhibition 'Peter Corrigan: Cities of Hope', 12 April – 8 June 2013.
10. Vlada Petric, *Construction in Film: The Man with the Movie Camera – A Cinematic Analysis*, Cambridge University Press (Cambridge), 1987, p 25.
11. Rowan Moore, 'The Art–Architecture Complex by Hal Foster – review', *Guardian*, 16 September 2011.
12. Philip Cox and John Maxwell Freeland, *Rude Timber Buildings in Australia*, Angus & Robertson (Sydney), 1980.
13. John Baldessari, *Painting for Kubler*, 2010: 'This painting owes its existence to prior paintings. By liking this solution, you should not be blocked in your continued acceptance of prior inventions. To attain this position, ideas of former painting had to be rethought.'
14. John Baldessari, *A Two-Dimensional Surface Without*

Any Articulation is a Dead Experience (1967) and *I Will Not Make Any More Boring Art* (1971).

15. Gwyn Jones, *Eirik the Red and Other Icelandic Sagas*, Oxford University Press (Oxford), 2008, p xi.

16. Andri Snær Magnason, *Dreamland: A Self-Help Manual for a Frightened Nation*, Citizen Press (London), 2008.

17. See Leon van Schaik, 'A conversation with Sean Godsell', in *El Croquis* no 165: *Sean Godsell 1997–2013*, Madrid, 2013, pp 6–18.

18. Leon van Schaik, 'Tides of Ambition: Who Architects Design For, and Who They Are When They Design',

in Geoffrey London (ed), *Momentum: New Victorian Architecture*, The Miegunyah Press (Melbourne), 2012, pp 42–52.

19. Gaston Bachelard, *The Poetics of Space* [*La Poétique de l'espace*, 1957], translated by Maria Jolas, Beacon Press (Boston, MA), 1969, p 8.

20. See Leon van Schaik, *Sean Godsell: Works and Projects*, Electa (Milan), 2004, pp 42–57 and 84–97.

21. See Geoffrey Scott, *The Architecture of Humanism*, University Paperbacks (London), 1961.

22. Michael Frayn, *The Human Touch*, Picador (New York), 2006, p 21.

23. Geoffrey MacNab, 'Robert

Redford and Wim Wenders on New Architecture Film *Cathedrals of Culture*', *The Independent*, 12 February 2014.

24. In conversation with the author at the opening of the building, 7 February 2014.

25. Peter Cook during his speech at the opening of the building, 7 February 2014.

26. Peter Cook, *Drawing: The Motive Force of Architecture*, Wiley (Chichester), 2008, p 21.

27. Cook 2008, p 9.

28. Cook 2008, p 201.

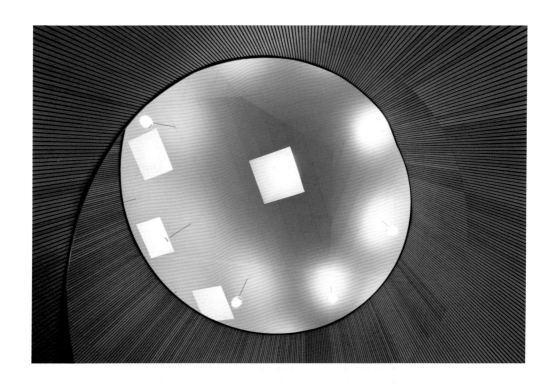

3

Healing
our City

The poetics in this chapter arises from architects being intent on making the richest possible conversations with the area of the city in which they are working. The practical impact of this poetics heals the city because it establishes connections across urban contexts, reweaving a fabric disrupted by the autonomy of modernist buildings by architects of previous generations. The heroics of that earlier period led architects and clients to feel no compunctions about ending conversations, lobbing onto sites autonomous bounded objects that were locked in a solipsistic conversation with themselves. The architects in this chapter have all found ways to create readable urban situations.

CZWG, Canada Water
Library, Southwark,
London, 2011

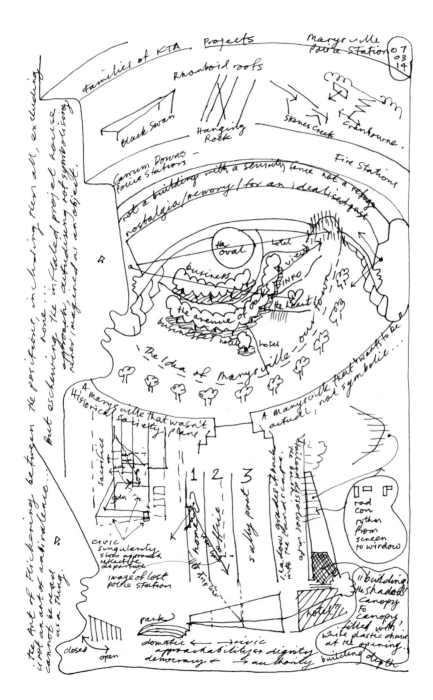

families of KTA Projects

Marysville Police Station 07 03 14

Rhomboid roofs

Black Swan

Hanging Rock

Skenes Creek

Cranbourne.

Carrum Downs — Police Stations

Fire Stations

not a building with a security fence not a refuge
nostalgia / memory / for an idealised past

the oval

hotel

views

business

INFO

the avenue of our business

the heart of town

hotel

hotel

The Idea of Marysville — our town...

A Marysville that wasn't Historical Society's place

A Marysville that wants to be actual, not symbolic...

1 2 3 sally port

sacrifice

open

civic
singularity
slow approach
reflect the
departure

image of lost
police station

house

office

shadow graded back
into the deliberate arc
open compositing out

rod
con
rythm
from
screen
to window

"building
the shadow
canopy
to canopy'
filled with
white plastic chairs
at the opening.

hotel

building depth

parks

closed → open

domestic ← → civic
approachability ↔ dignity
democracy ← → authority

the Art of Flickering between the positive, including plan all, excluding none...
But eschewing the inflated project house approach, advocating not symbolising, rather imagined as an object.
i not an art of ambivalence... cannot be read as a thing.

Community Police Station, Marysville, Victoria, Australia[1]

Kerstin Thompson Architects (KTA), 2012

The architect here worked with a community recovering after a catastrophic forest fire. She honoured memories of the past without symbolising them, and expressed democratic approachability while providing the contemporary actuality of a civic presence in a small town. She drew the poetics of her response from her evolving practice.

Marysville is a small town located in the southerly foothills of the Great Dividing Range that separates East Coast Australia from the hinterland. A great arc of mature oak trees curves down past a park that channels views to Lake Mountain (the nearest ski slope) towards a cricket and football oval in the bowl of a valley, and there are views to often snow-covered peaks beyond. After the catastrophic fires of 2009, almost all that survived of the town was this arc of oaks and the smooth turf of the oval, and the views to the peaks are to silhouettes of pencil-slender trunks of the burned mountain ash forest.

After the catastrophe there were those who moved away, determined not to return, and those who stayed, determined to rebuild the town and honour its history. Framework plans were devised, reflecting the simple identity of the town. Reconstruction commenced – houses, small hotels, shops and cafés more or less as they had been, in a quasi-vernacular. Flanking the downhill edge of the park, another architect has designed a neo-*Learning from Las Vegas* information centre, a shed-like form proclaiming in large letters MARYSVILLE.[2] Eventually the community decided that it was appropriate to locate the lost police station on the uphill flank of the park, creating a civic cluster.

But there were concerns. One Las Vegas was enough, thought some; a fenced compound was feared; the park had become the focus of Arcadian memories that needed to be protected; and rebuilding to the historical plans was a sentimental favourite, but the nature and scope of policing had changed to become more about daily community service – lost property and counselling – and occasional disaster management. There was a suspicion about solutions being imposed from the city a two- to three-hour drive away across the ranges.

Leon van Schaik, research ideogram, 7 March 2014
Drawn at the conclusion of researching the project.

Architects KTA were appointed. Having previously completed a number of community and larger police stations, as well as fire stations, they were

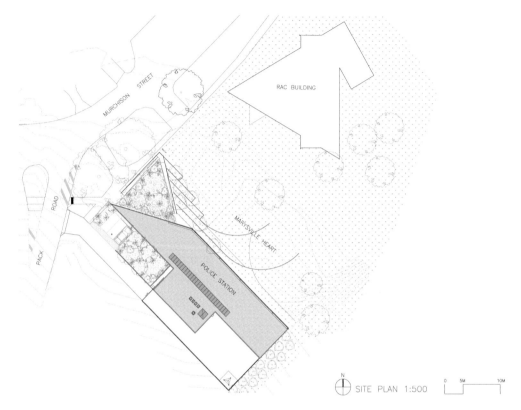

MURCHISON STREET

RAC BUILDING

ROAD

PACK

MARYSVILLE HEART

POLICE STATION

N

SITE PLAN 1:500

0   5M   10M

equipped with experience of the nuances of uniformed cultures with their alternating routines of waiting and then of dynamic action. In addition, the practice has grown from working on individual houses, and developed an ear for hearing the unspoken, the unstated hopes and fears of clients. Perhaps their most significant civic project to date is their visitors centre for the Royal Botanic Gardens at Cranbourne (2009), a building that gently and almost imperceptibly, through its siting and thoughtful arrangement of programme, gives visitors an overview before they descend down meticulously calibrated ramps and stairs into the gardens themselves. The houses have developed a language of rectangular roofs angled and tilted to admit and exclude sunlight and capture views. Families of approaches have built up, and at Marysville these learnings parade onto the stage.

As in some other projects, the programme is analysed abstractly, not function by function, but in zones running from the intimate and personal to the

Kerstin Thompson Architects, Community Police Station, Marysville, Victoria, Australia, 2012
Site plan showing the triangle of the information centre at the top, the park between it and the Police Station at the bottom.

formal and public and the formal and private. These zones run in parallel, growing in width as they progress across the site. In a move first identified in the ladies' lounge of Adolf Loos's Müller House in Prague (1930),[3] a view cone from the most removed and intimate place to that of public arrival is established, here running from a tea-making sink with a domestic view into the park, through a common room area, to a wall made translucent by a pixelated photograph of the old police station, to the enquiry desk.

The rhomboidal roof, as in many KTA projects, does much of the work of scaling the spaces across the zonal gradient, here running from a low point at the rear to the east. Along the northeast face of the building the eaves are tucked down onto a paling wall made of radially cut timbers fanning out to become window mullions, closing up to form screens. As the ground falls away northwards, the wall sits on a series of contour walls that step down towards the oak-lined street. This part of the site has been made over to the park, and the subtly rhythmical wall does the duty of the much-feared fence. The roof rises up towards the southern boundary of the site, where it terminates on the solid walls of the sally port (enclosed entrance court) with undisguised finality. The service areas of a new hotel next door will back onto this.

Kerstin Thompson Architects, Community Police Station, Marysville, Victoria, Australia, 2012
Plan showing the lateral layering of the programme. Staff standing at the tea kitchen at the indent to the north look into the park created outside, and can see through to the reception counter to the left.

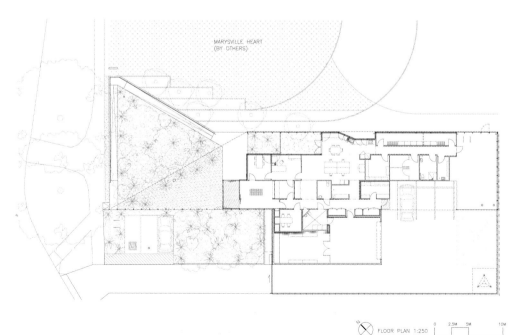

MARYSVILLE HEART
(BY OTHERS)

FLOOR PLAN 1:250

At the midpoint, though, the roof at the rear covers a yard where the palings are just that – a timber fence to the park – and the planting has already overshot the domestic scale of the building as seen from this side. And to the street front, the roof is pulled across to the site boundary and then cut back at a sharp angle to the park edge. This over-sailing roof, supported on a cylindrical column on its north edge and on vertical steel struts along its southwestern edge, which flash between being a solid and then a permeable screen as you walk past, 'builds shadow' and grades the project back into the site, creating a canopy that links into that of the oaks that line the street. This open space serves as a verandah sheltering from sun and rain, as it did at the opening ceremony when it was filled with white plastic chairs, though more usually it provides casual respite.

The street is falling to the northeast, and the forecourt of the station is faced with a slowly rising wall running against the slope. Along this rises the ramp to the front door, which runs to the northeast limit of the site and then cuts

Kerstin Thompson Architects, Community Police Station, Marysville, Victoria, Australia, 2012
Interior view of the tea kitchen looking out to the park.

Kerstin Thompson
Architects, Community
Police Station, Marysville,
Victoria, Australia, 2012
The civic scale of the canopy
as seen from the entrance.
A single cylindrical column
supports it on one side, and
closely spaced vertical steel
struts on the other.

(Following page) Kerstin
Thompson Architects,
Community Police Station,
Marysville, Victoria,
Australia, 2012
View from the oak-lined
street showing the civic
canopy to the left and the
sally port to the right.

(Following page) Kerstin
Thompson Architects,
Community Police Station,
Marysville, Victoria,
Australia, 2012
Long view from the park
showing how the building
almost becomes a paling
fence at the left and how
the roof rises to the right to
form the civic canopy on the
oak-lined street edge.

back to the low paling wall side of the building, revealing a curve of space
that has been given to the park. This raised garden sets up an arena overview
of the Marysville Heart, as the park is called, creating a gradually intensifying
sense of civic separation. Perhaps this is how civic dignity is best conveyed.
The slow angled ramp and a set of stepping stones that run directly to the
door give a duality of arrival and departure modes: rapid and reflective, an

invention first used at Cranbourne, and one that seems in itself to signal the various modes of the civic use of the station.

Companion to Community Police Station: John Wardle Architects, Rokeby Street Studio and redevelopment, Collingwood, Victoria, Australia, 2013
The brick warehouse was converted into studios. These extend into the metal-clad annexe that mediates with the graffiti-covered corrugated-iron warehouse next door. A café at street level is an unlikely tenancy in this former industrial area, but has become a cultural hub for the creative industries.

This is strange, because there is no ambiguity here. We are not reading domestic approachability at one moment, and civic duty at another, but a constant flickering between the two, as if the building were saying that we cannot have the one without the other, and that we live on a gradient between the two, just as the lone policeman who on quiet days makes tea and looks out into the garden, and on rare occasions musters with colleagues to deal with emergencies or with a serious felony.

This marshalling of the poetics of this spectrum of life, from the mundane to the dramatic, has emerged from many years of designing across this spectrum, and is won largely from the cauldron of family life housed in an extreme and difficult climate and terrain.

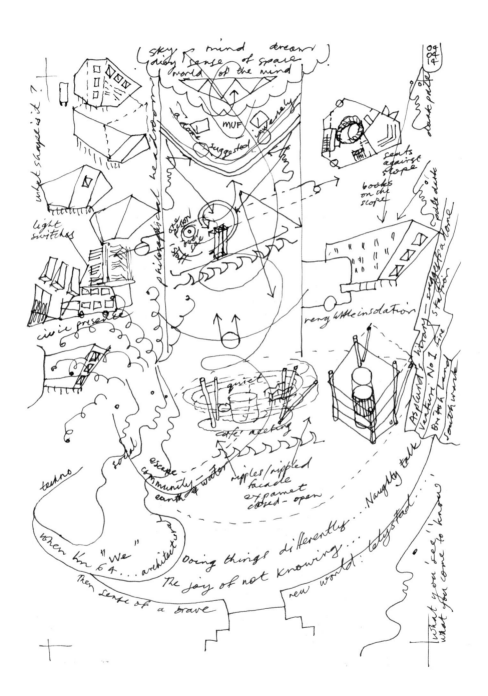

Canada Water Library, Surrey Quays, Southwark, London

CZWG, 2011

In this project the architect Piers Gough describes how he uses 'naughty talk' to propose unthinkable ideas and how he uses this naughtiness to win people over to support his design. His upending of the expected produces a deceptively simple poetics that on close examination reconciles complexities of site and programme into a readily graspable spatial design.

'You are one in a million!' declares a banner that stands between sofas in the entrance area of the Canada Water Library; 'You are our millionth visitor since we opened in November 2011, one of an average of a thousand per day'. Opposite it, across the timber floor, is a café with tables overlooking the water of the docks to the south. The banner is midway between the two revolving door entries – one to the southwest alongside the stairs to the Underground station, the other to the north and facing the civic

plaza of what (given all the new apartment buildings, a bus station and the Underground) could be a new city on new ground; a Dutch polder settlement, perhaps. There is just enough remnant dock of the old Surrey Quays to suggest an urban palimpsest, but at first sight there is nothing to lead you to expect that this building need take anything other than its own organisational requirements into account.

So contemplating the banner at the base of a cylinder of space up which coils a slow-rising, easily trafficable stair, there is this comfortable sense that you are in a rectangular foyer, with photocopy and print machines to one side, toilets and the café servery opposite, facing its seating area, and lifts obliquely adjacent. A warm buzz of activity under an orange ceiling, with only a set of bookshelves carved into the wall of the cylinder to suggest a library. But the void soars upwards, timber fluted, and above it there is a floating form bouncing light in unexpected directions.

Take the stairs – so friendly that people with sticks take them in preference to the lifts, and something obviously 'library' happens. Satisfying your

CZWG, Canada Water Library, Southwark, London, 2011
On the library floor, users arrive at a single control point whether they use either the stairs (the most popular option) or the lifts (just to the left of the head of the stairs). The book stacks snake away towards workstations at peripheral windows; the children's library is beyond the control point. Note the pendulous ceiling punctured with rooflights – an inverse dome effect. At the top right there is a glimpse of the mezzanine workstations that ring the library floor.

expectations, it gets quieter and quieter as you rise, until the buzz below is only a visual fragment seen through the lens of the cylinder. Your head emerges above the balustrade and you are in library-world, facing the control desk – as are those who have come up by lift. This is a double-volume space lined at its perimeter by thin columns, some at an angle, ambiguously defining a space that has mushroomed magically in area and shape as you rise through the cylinder. Bookcases snake away in zigzags, and windows give hanging views out to the water and to the plaza. The ceiling cones down to press on the top of the central-seeming stair bulging into the space.

The architect for the project is Piers Gough, a founding director of the unusual commercial practice CZWG. The partners Nicholas Campbell, Roger Zogolovitch, Rex Wilkinson and Piers Gough studied at the Architectural Association in London between 1965 and 1971 and they formed the practice in 1975, developing two streams of work: converting buildings into studios for creative industry professionals, and finding unusual sites that could house apartment buildings for a new generation of people who wanted to live in the inner city. Appealing to these clients, their designs are considered 'funky' – as the cartoon shows.

Over the years the firm has won the respect of developers, one of which, Lend Lease, made appointing CZWG as the architects a condition of their providing Southwark Council with the site for the library. Thus, the commission, arriving when he was 64, was Piers Gough's first institutional building. As we go around the library, Piers affirms that the ceiling design was inspired by a project by the architectural practice muf that had a ceiling moulded into shape by a mass of water. Here this was achieved by flipping the roof truss. So it is that the shallow underside of this hanging form seems to shoot up over a perimeter mezzanine

Louis Hellman, sketch of CZWG founding partners, 1988
From left to right: Nicholas Campbell, Roger Zogolovitch, Rex Wilkinson and Piers Gough.

English Extremists~

study-gallery, evident to you now that you see that it is lined with studying heads. Once up on the mezzanine, reached directly by the gangway stair, the pendulous ceiling arrests cross-views and directs them down to the central cylinder. No one ends up staring at someone else who is studying. And the space mushrooms again, with a series of seminar and meeting rooms lining the south and east edges of the building.

This is a Tardis library. What seemed a simple rectangular footprint at ground level has grown at every storey, and the shape of the plan eludes us as the functions array themselves ever more comfortably in space. What we need to know is clear in our minds: the warm social interactions of the ground level, and the rise up the timber fluted cylinder towards the floating cloud of the roof, punctured with a quasi-circle of rooflights that suggest a dome, in the same way (as Piers agrees) as Erik Gunnar Asplund, in his Stockholm Library (1928), suggested the dome he could not afford by square-scalloping his central brick cylinder. In doing this, says Piers, you rise out of the realm of the community into the world of the mind, of dreams, of things no one in your community would ever tell you about, as Piers told the community reference group in what he calls his 'naughty talk' – a talk that won them over.

CZWG, Canada Water Library, Southwark, London, 2011
Model with the internal floors lifting out, revealing how the canted form of the building contains the floors that grow in plan area from the ground floor to the top mezzanine, and hangs out over Surrey Quays progressively.

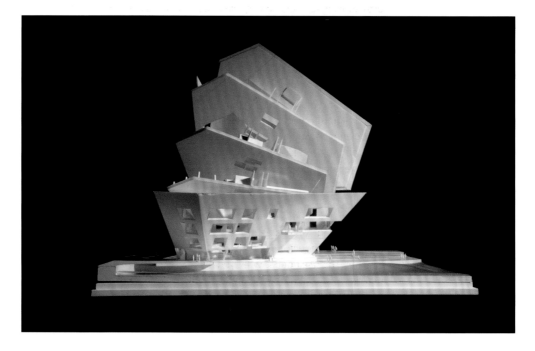

Easy. But wait. The building plan footprint is very small and tightly constrained by the Jubilee line below, by the civic plaza masterplanned over it with view corridors to Canada Water, and by the edge of the old dock. This gives a tight six-sided figure. The brief for the library doubled in area as the scale of the development around it sank in, and even so it is serving double that projected number of visits. The library client had in mind a stack of book floors; Piers asked whether they might prefer one floor, arguing that the secret to a library open all hours is that it is easily staffed and monitored by a single librarian, and he showed how, through progressively fattening out the plan by projecting outwards, he could achieve a library with the spatial unity of the one Alvar Aalto designed for the German city of Wolfsburg (1962), although organised by rising upwards, not sinking into the ground. What is more, the resulting overhangs reduce insolation to make this a very energy efficient building.

Still easy. A central organising form, the cylinder, spikes through from a tight ground floor into a double-volume library surrounded by a mezzanine study-gallery with seminar rooms hanging off behind them. But wait! What, set below those marching two-storey bay windows that look like light switches, is that red, double-height pair of fire-station doors facing the piazza to the north, looking (as Piers agrees) like Robert Venturi's Fire Station Number 4 in Columbus, Indiana (1968)? And what are those double doors in the foyer, leading off behind the cylinder? There is a ghost floor here! Into this projects the double-volume 'Black Box' theatre (Piers made it theatrical red and provided windows to the south for rehearsal days) that is tucked into the southeast corner of the building, the leaning angles of the facade supporting a raking chevron of seats. The lower parts of the bay windows serve a staff room that in turn gives on to a south-facing work area with its own balcony overlooking the water. The rising cylinder takes its time to shift you out of the business of daily life and into the realm of the mind; a full storey of space is elided as you walk up into the cylinder, lined with masses of acoustic absorbents, quietly rising through stretched time and space.

Everything that seems simple here has been hard won by fiendishly clever spatial thinking. It is enabled by a flat plate slab supported on columns at its periphery, a structural system that allows the flowing disposition of plan elements. This itself defies what you expect: you assume that the lifts and the toilet/escape stacks support the concrete slabs of the floors. They do not – that work is done by the fringe of pipe columns in splayed and upright couplets and triplets. Even at its most artfully material, Piers's thinking surprises when you see what is exactly there. The skin of the building ripples;

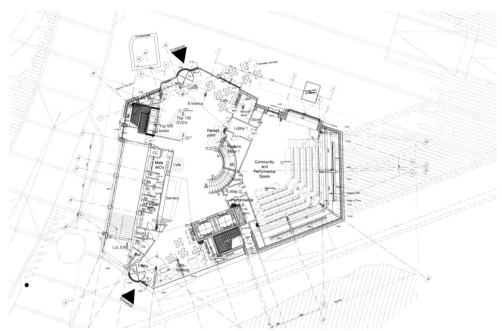

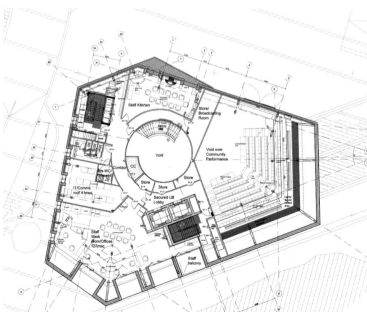

CZWG, Canada Water Library, Southwark, London, 2011
Six-sided figure of the ground floor plan with exit from the Underground station to the left, amphitheatre to the right and café along the left, down to the south entrance and copy centre near the north entrance.

CZWG, Canada Water Library, Southwark, London, 2011
Plan of the floor that is not reached by the grand central staircase. A void over the amphitheatre to the bright library offices and restrooms to the left.

CZWG, Canada Water Library, Southwark, London, 2011
Plan of the library level: staff point between the lifts and the top of the stair; children's library to the lower left; book stacks to the right.

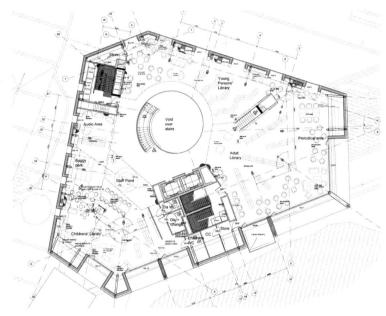

CZWG, Canada Water Library, Southwark, London, 2011
The top-level library mezzanine, showing study spaces along the balcony edge and meeting rooms behind along the building perimeter, each side of the lifts and services.

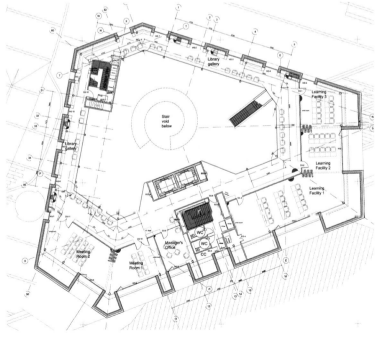

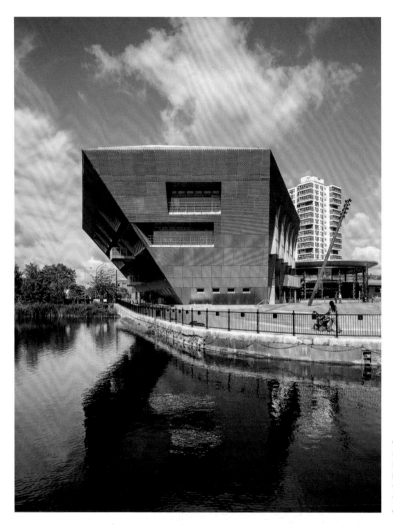

CZWG, Canada Water
Library, Southwark,
London, 2011
From this angle, the elusive
form of the building is seen
to involve a larger overhang
above the remaining dock.

of course it does – it is at Canada Water, so any casual popular thinking will
lead you to 'ripple', will it not? But look again. On site Piers shows that the
building is clad in a material made by cutting slots into bronze-anodised
aluminium sheets and expanding those holes. Designing it, Piers asked if
the expansion could be graduated in stages, from a mere depression to
fully opened out; surprised, as they had never been asked this before, the
manufactures said that it could. So at ground level there are no actual cuts in
the metal sheathing, and as Piers says: 'you cannot stick a cigarette stub in'.[4]

So it is that when you are close to the building it looks pale at the base and dark at the eaves, diminishing its scale. But unexpectedly and fortuitously, when seen from a distance this reverses, and the building takes its place as a large ship-like mass in this assemblage of urban pieces, and sets off the double-decker buses that sweep past its western face every few minutes. It has the air of being moored here.

Piers talks of 'the joy of not knowing, of doing things differently'. He delights in 'naughty talk', which airs what he 'not knows' and opens the way for his prodigious spatial thinking to come into play, as it does in this surprising building, one that you assume you understand at a glance. But, as so many architectural tourists (and indeed I myself) have discovered on emerging from the Underground and being unable to find the building because it lurks behind you like your own turtle shell, this is a building that you cannot assume that you understand.

This was a landmark project marking the new civic heart of a large housing development. The developer sought a remarkable outcome, and hence arranged for CZWG to be appointed architects. Southwark Council were however the client; they had a limited budget and a tightly prescribed functional brief. Like any public building, the library had to provide universal access, such that no one was disadvantaged. As described above, Piers worked hard to win over the client, and found a great ally in the librarians.

Companion to Canada Water Library: Martine de Maeseneer Architects, Bronks Youth Theatre, Brussels, 2005
Situated in a heritage area, the architects negotiated between the cultural expectations of the Flemish and Walloon communities, and achieved a modest presence on the street by creating top lit basement areas.

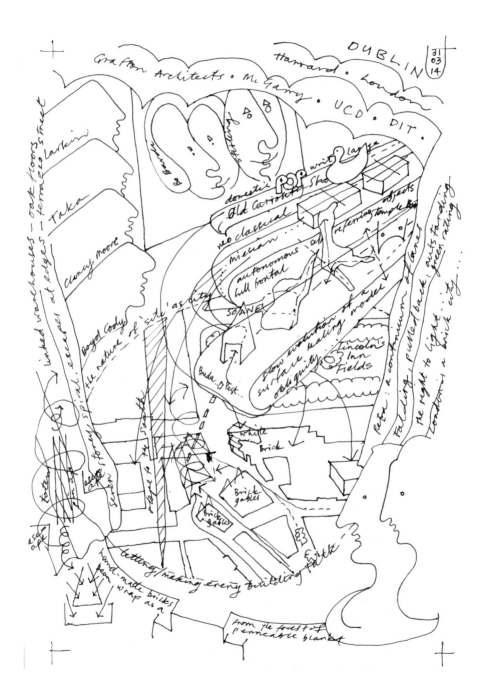

DUBLIN 31/03/14

Grafton Architects • McGarry • Harvard • London • UCD • DIT •

Saw Swee Hock Student Centre, London School of Economics and Political Science (LSE), London

O'Donnell + Tuomey, 2014

Communities of practice in architecture and the architectural cultures that they nurture provide sustaining mental space to a practice. From their home base in Ireland, a country with a compact architectural community, architects Sheila O'Donnell and John Tuomey have developed a unique approach to healing city fabric, creating poetic continuums of space and materiality.

How do architectural cultures grow? On parabolas, we might say, following Andrei Voznesensky – architecture student turned poet and keen observer of creative processes – as we observe our protagonists crash through places and generations, taking what is, after all, the quickest way there.[5] Where? In the case of the Irish practice O'Donnell + Tuomey, the parabola takes them from Dublin to London and the Saw Swee Hock Student Centre at the London School of Economics and Political Science (LSE). Their first London commission was the Photographers' Gallery in Soho (2012), a project in which they winnowed out of an existing building an architectural nobility reminiscent of the work of the De Stijl movement in the Netherlands (1917–1931). Evidenced here in their second major commission in London is the latest assemblage of a poetics built up through many projects in brick in Ireland, especially Timberyard Social Housing (Dublin, 2009) and the Lyric Theatre (Belfast, 2011).

London is the city in which – at the other end of their parabola –Sheila O'Donnell and John Tuomey began their post-graduating explorations under the influence of James Stirling. They have crashed back into the English capital as members of a generation of Dublin architects whose practices were forged in the architectural healing of Temple Bar, a turning point in the history of a city that up until that point – driven (not alas for the last time) by a ruthless development ethic – appeared to be spiralling into aphasic dissolution. A well-trodden path (Dublin–London–Dublin …) took them back from the glory days of Stirling's Neue Staatsgalerie in Stuttgart (1984) to work with their peers on a series of projects in the medieval core of their own city. Here, on sites reached by small and winding lanes, they learned how to set large, initially Stirlingesque, figures to work obliquely.

Leon van Schaik, research ideogram, 31 March 2014 Drawn at the conclusion of researching the project.

Glimpsed at an angle, these suggested a large ambition, but never presented it as anything other than a fleeting possibility, fleshed out fully only on the occasion of early or late light soaking in across luscious red brickwork. The two architects became adept at suggesting continuums of every kind: drawing streets into their foyers, and re-energising the surviving brick fabric around their projects by formally matching its motifs in their own brickwork forms. From importing a Euro-style language, they moved to an architecture that talked to and of every neighbour, to a history and to a future for each site.

Even in less charged situations, up arterial roads, and working with tightly circumscribed housing briefs, they would scoop up the full length of an existing red-brick boundary wall and a row of red-brick terraces along a lane

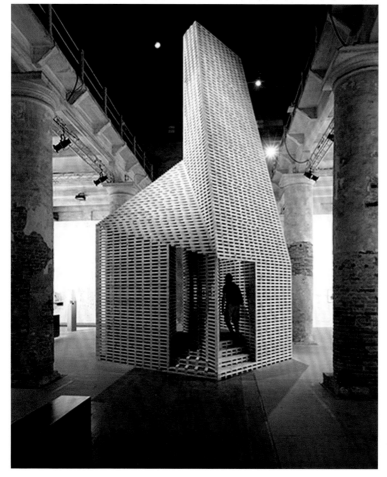

O'Donnell + Tuomey, *Vessel*, 'Common Ground' exhibition, Venice Architecture Biennale, 2012
At the exhibition, the large-scale model enticed visitors into its welcoming form.

at right angles to the thoroughfare, and wind these into the composition of a mother block and a child block of apartments that shielded a new courtyard from the busy road and made all benefit, the old recognised as an integral part of a larger new to which it seemed the germ, the new validated by its seeming to grow out of the old. A continuum of dwelling made manifest in form and material. In Belfast, on the flanks of a river, they coiled the programme for the Lyric Theatre down the hill, so that it begins at the scale of the surrounding suburban red-brick houses and then turns slowly to present to the water's edge the civic dignity of a major cultural institution, not looking like a transplant but seemingly grown from a graft. A carving out of city blocks is underway in Budapest, at the Central European University, where this process is at work in reverse, excavating and removing matter as spaces and faces are reawakened and brought back into the city consciousness.

O'Donnell + Tuomey, Saw Swee Hock Student Centre, LSE, London, 2014 Drawing showing the design of a corner between two flanks of the brick blanket to the Student Centre.

The craft of doing this, the thinking and making of it, is overtly and concretely experimental. Models are made. And remade. One, *Vessel* (2012),

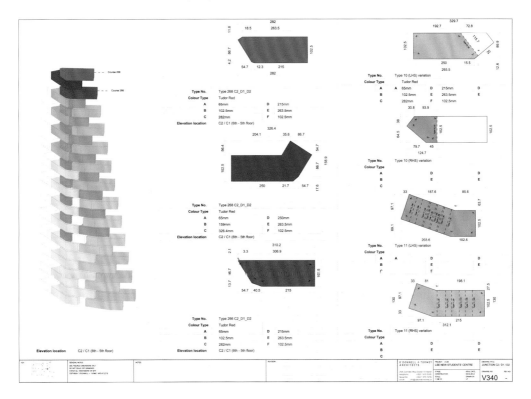

started in the office as an exploration of ways to enter a building and was scaled up to allow visitors to walk through it. Constructed out of interlocking timber, it was included in the 'Common Ground' exhibition at the 2012 Venice Architecture Biennale. Bricks and brick patterns are studied, tested and exhibited too. The designing is in conversation with a wide community of practice.

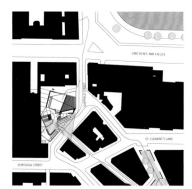

O'Donnell + Tuomey, Saw Swee Hock Student Centre, LSE, London, 2014
Site plan revealing the urban grain that the design engages, reconnecting with several generations of development. The autonomous blocks of the 1970s are to the right, off the page. The 16th-century Old Curiosity Shop is in the crooked finger of the top right figure.

At the LSE, this evolution of poetic thinking reaches an apogee. The continuum thinking is there: gables and brick faces of surrounding buildings all join forces with the Vorticist swirling of a folded brick 'blanket' that drapes the angles of allowable development of a leftover site at the head of a tangle of narrow streets.

Earlier LSE planners were intent on destroying the medieval lanes by imposing on them large rationalist self-contained figure buildings that muscle in without so much as a by-your-leave to their neighbours. For some years around the LSE, brick buildings have lost their conversation as concrete lumps have crowded into this city area, with beetling arched skylines threatening to bury the work of centuries past. Thanks to O'Donnell + Tuomey's new building, brick buildings all around, including Sir John Soane's Museum on the opposite side of Lincoln's Inn Fields to the north, have re-joined the city chatter. Talking architecture rescued in the nick of time.

How is this done? There is a complex meshing of needs-must and romantic Petra-inspired picturesque reverse-designing of vistas up narrow defiles, mapping sight lines up narrow streets, allowing the set-backs required by 'rights to light' and best-practice environmental design.

The angling of the faces, the pulling back from the rear edge of the site and the visual conjoining with the brick flanks of the former London Research Institute (1962) have the effect of diminishing the new building's apparent scale, and the 16th-century Old Curiosity Shop is triumphantly set within this frame with a renewed authority, as its stepping out seems to charge the Student Centre's stepping back.

O'Donnell + Tuomey,
Saw Swee Hock Student
Centre, LSE, London, 2014
The 'blanket' of brickwork
works to reduce the
apparent scale of the mass
and to frame and foreground
existing brick structures
around it. Note the large
canopy: this creates an
external room.

The site approximates to a double-square rectangle running north–south, with the southern square cut back almost to the diagonal. Fire escape stairs are tucked into the southwest corner and halfway across the angled-to-the-south northern face. It is as if huge brick curtains, lacy in areas, have been hung from these, draping down the rear northwestern face and jagging across the southeastern face. Swirling up in the middle is the lift shaft, a highly coloured totem pole around which the lanes outside, invited in spiral upwards – a movement skewered in place below by a downward corkscrewing concrete circular stair and held up to the sky above by the sudden reappearance of the same massive concrete screw.

The brief was to bring student facilities together under one roof. The multifunctional building includes a multipurpose hall, pub, learning café, media centre, prayer room, offices, gym, careers office, dance studio and social spaces. Every part of the building's programme argued for a face to the

street, and so it is that a terrazzo street comes in over the large basement
black box – which has its connection to the street outside through a huge
clerestory light, and to the rear courtyards through further such lights – and
goes on up past the learning café, the media centre with its table for banner
making, the multi-faith centre with its miniature Aaltoesque brick drum
chapel, to the student union offices, the gym and finally to a rooftop café
with an external terrace looking back into Lincoln's Inn Fields.

The conceit of a blanket or a curtain holds true because the bricks run from
top to bottom, the lacy areas covering windows, while floor levels are all
obscured. The curtains do not fold or wave wilfully. Perspex negative models
of all the constraints were used to test the design as it evolved. The brief
had the aspiration for an 'excellent' green building rating. Thanks in part to
these brick screens, which help to bring daylight into every space, the design
achieved the higher 'outstanding' rating. But this is also a very theatrical
structure. Every sketch and model demonstrates how the angles of the curtain
are being tweaked to give the maximum drama to the views into and out of

the building. These sketches and models show how the building was made to 'talk' to and about all of its neighbours.

O'Donnell + Tuomey, Saw Swee Hock Student Centre, LSE, London, 2014 Drawing showing the internal street spiralling around the upward-urging triangles of the graphic on the central 'totem pole' of the lift shafts.

So here – as ever since Temple Bar – O'Donnell + Tuomey assert the theatricality of the city, of buildings themselves. There is here a claim for the city and its buildings as the absolutely necessary setting for our fleeting lives, our pursuits of our desires and our understandings. The brief called for the best student building in the United Kingdom. It is hard to know how such a result could be judged. Maybe this is pulling a long bow, but as I watch people under the generous canopy, pausing to gather themselves before they resume their day, I do not think so: I see here how Dublin yet again is the source for our contemporary appreciation of the role of the city fabric in our lives. This is a conversational designing that comes out of James Joyce's *Ulysses* (1922), that stream of consciousness in Dublin.[6]

Companion to Saw Swee Hock Student Centre: Searle x Waldron Architecture, Annexe to the Art Gallery of Ballarat, Victoria, Australia, 2011 Nick Searle and Suzannah Waldron used this opportunity to fill in an elbow and create new continuities with dislocated pieces of the historic city core.

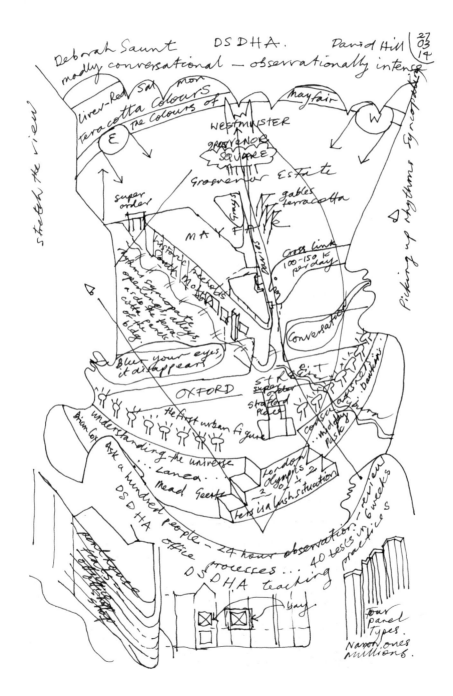

South Molton Street Building, London

DSDHA, 2012

Deborah Saunt of DSDHA uses techniques of close observation, bringing many eyes to bear on project issues, going out into the street to ask a hundred people what they think. Compiling rich ('thick') descriptions, these architects create a conversational poetics in the city, but one that has the edginess of a new idea.

As our understandings of the universe shift, as our views about consciousness change and as our understandings of our own anthropology alter, we view the city in new ways – ways that differ sometimes starkly from those of previous generations. What passes for 'close observation' in one generation is myopia to the next generation.[7] Observing ourselves observing has become the contemporary way in which traps of the past are avoided – if indeed avoiding those traps is our goal. You might think it was no longer possible for architects to argue for the autonomy of the architectural object, but those who produce closed-boundary objects still long for the totalitarian political conditions that brought such horror to the 20th century.[8] Such views persisted as a bad hangover in the slab-and-beam perimeter blocks, alien objects that were dropped into cities everywhere in the post-Second World

DSDHA, South Molton Street Building, London, 2012
Overall view of the building in its context, showing the buildings it 'converses' with.

Leon van Schaik, research ideogram, 27 March 2014
Drawn at the conclusion of researching the project.

DSDHA, South Molton Street Building, London, 2012
One 'discussion' pairs a large first-floor window with another in the building immediately adjacent to the left, seen to the left of the kiosk in the foreground.

DSDHA, South Molton Street Building, London, 2012
The curved shop window at the nose of the building, and those above, reassert the presence of the site, nudging towards Oxford Street and signalling Mayfair behind. The human scale of the ground-floor windows, usually occupied by a mannequin, seems to attract people. There is almost always someone photographing this view.

War years. Perhaps these are best understood through analysing the conversations that these buildings embed. Like the blob architecture of the present, these are designs that talk only to themselves, as if they are disconnected from the world, from the universe.

London-based architects Deborah Saunt and David Hills founded their practice DSDHA doing educational buildings, kindergartens, schools and a university building in Cambridge. As architects they are a superb exemplar of the nascent and opposing approach: their buildings are, as Deborah puts it, 'madly conversational', chatting to everything around them, past and present, and in this – unlike the purveyors of autonomy who seek to crush all other voices – they reconstitute a city that trusts what people are saying, have said or might yet say.

DSDHA, South Molton Street Building, London, 2012
Practice design conversations begin with a sketch. This drawing conveys the key moves made in forming the concept of a building that frames a conversation with the surrounding buildings and streets.

In early spring, lavender flowers profusely on the upper floors of DSDHA's commercial development at the tip of South Molton Street, and the colour seems to flow down the flanks of the building as it noses out of the complex lanes of Mayfair into the shopping thoroughfare of Oxford Street. The facades of the building collect the impulses of small freehold developments along that street and between Bond Street to the east and Davies Street to the west, and then launches northwards across Oxford Street into a dialogue with Stratford Place, one of London's first conscious urban figures.

DSDHA, South Molton Street Building, London, 2012
Profiles of the terracotta cladding that articulates the facade and makes colour links to surrounding buildings.

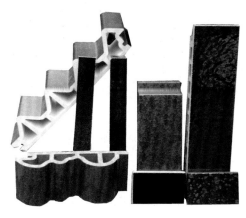

How does it do this? The building reclaims the full extent of its flatiron site, making a basement beneath the pavements and occupying with two storeys each of shop, office and of residential space right up to the apex of the triangle, concluding at the tightest possible circumference of curved glass. The building bulges out in bays towards Oxford Street, thus setting up a super-order gateway to Mayfair.

The skin of the building is vertically striated with terracotta panels in four widths and with differing profiles, and horizontal sills separate the functions. Thin panels serve as mullions to the glazing; wider ones form the solid walls. These panels are syncopated so that, when seen obliquely – which they mostly are – they re-create the vertical rhythms of the facades down the full length of the street.

A pattern of piano nobile grand openings in bays is picked up from the full street facade and incorporated. As the building swings round into Davies Street, a plain base below the South Molton Street level tapers along the fall in the road, and a half-level difference at the corner with South Molton Lane is used to form a foyer to the access to the offices and flat. Here on the turn, the fluting and set-backs are muted and a tower form emerges, matching that of the gabled rear of the Browns fashion store, an Edwardian terracotta confection. At the top of this tower a balcony is notched in, hinting at the views to Berkeley Square and Westminster Abbey beyond. This tower also bookends the views up the laneways between Davies Street and South Molton Street.

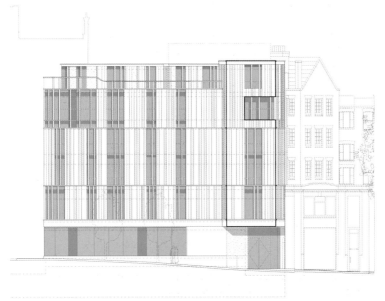

DSDHA, South Molton Street Building, London, 2012
Elevation to Davies Street, showing how the slope of the street is used to locate an entry half a level down.

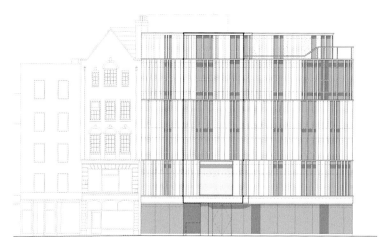

DSDHA, South Molton Street Building, London, 2012
Elevation to South Molton Street, showing how the large opening on the second level relates to the large window in the building to the left.

This immensely subtle but powerful composition was designed in six weeks, due to a break clause in the lease agreement that enabled redevelopment, and when construction commenced the building had a strict limit established by the client who wanted to be trading by the 2012 Olympic Games. Even so, in this tight time-frame, around forty designs were modelled and tested as the early sketches were developed.

Of course the concept did not emerge cold. Through the years of establishing an office and teaching culture that demands that sites in the city be approached through wide interrogation of subdivision and facade patterns, that at regular intervals the designers go out into the street and 'ask a hundred people', and that all of these observations be presented and reviewed by the whole office or studio, DSDHA is set up to respond with accurate and incisive observations of actualities past, present and future.

The patterning of the facades was complemented by a paving proposal that swept a trafficable arc up the hill from Davies Street and round into South Molton Street – this is a hill that at its base will accept some 150,000 people a day when the Crossrail station opens. That design led to the design of the paving of the entire street, a reinforcement of syncopations between minor openings to shops and major openings to passages and alleys.

The terracotta panels themselves reflect what is a predominant material in Mayfair, and one that is gloriously present in the mouldings and details of

DSDHA, South Molton
Street Building, London,
2012
A sample of the forty or so
iterations of the design that
were developed and tested.

the Grays Antique Centre down along Davies Street. A liver-red colour was
developed that spoke to the salmon pinks and the deep reds in the urban
scene in which the building is set.

'Blur your eyes,' says Deborah, 'and the building disappears.' The design
gives meaning to the term 'urban fabric' – this is made of the stuff of this
part of Mayfair; intellectually made, in that there is no mimicry but rather
a deep understanding that informs a new technical approach to building
within a respected historical frame. This is a building that people love to
photograph: it delights and surprises, so people respond and, a little surprised
at themselves, they join the conversation.

Recently Deborah and David have been designing a house for themselves –
the Covert House (2014) in Clapham, southwest London. As we shall see,
there are a number of reasons for naming it 'covert'. As in all their projects,
intense research (here into creating a site in and under the gardens between
two rows of terraced houses – hence 'covert') led to sketches. But, feeling
that this was a private work, their own house, these sketches stayed on the
kitchen table and did not make the journey into the conversation space of

Companion to the
South Molton Street
Building: Lyons, Swanston
Academic Building, RMIT,
Melbourne, 2012
The seeming playfulness
of this enormously popular
building is structured around
an intense observation and
conversation with its urban
surroundings.

the office. It remained 'covert'. The design languished, and in analysing the
projects of DSDHA, Deborah was startled to find that she ranked this project
very low against all of her quality indicators. This puzzled and annoyed
her, and then she decided to take the project, quite literally, into the office,
where it became part of the conversational structure that she and David have
crafted there. There were office and teaching unit site visits, and the project
entered the regime of design reviews, eliciting comments and suggestions
from all. And life came into the project. It has been completed, and is happily
occupied. This anecdote delivers the message about the DSDHA poetics: it
flourishes in acute and articulate conversation, verbal and visual, within a
community of practice and teaching, and with sites in the broad.

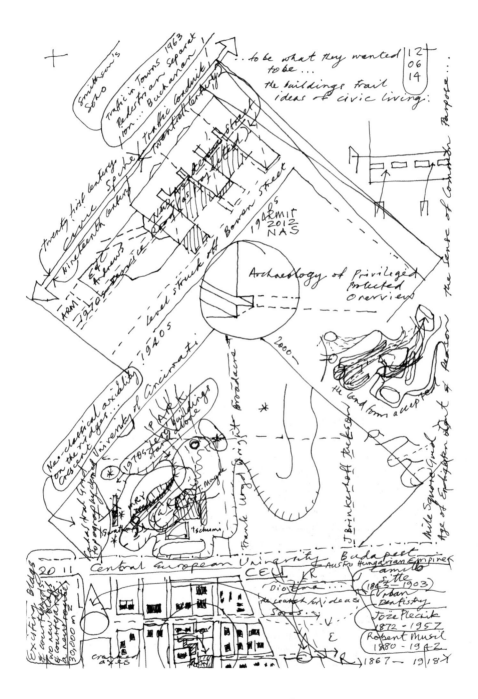

Leon van Schaik, research
ideogram, 12 June 2014
Drawn at the conclusion of
researching the project.

Three University Makeovers:

University of Cincinnati Masterplan, Cincinnati, Ohio

Hargreaves Associates, 2000

Central European University remodelling, Budapest

O'Donnell + Tuomey, 2011

RMIT New Academic Street, Melbourne

Lyons with NMBW Architecture Studio, Minifie van Schaik Architects (MvS), Harrison and White (HAW) and Maddison Architects, 2014

These projects deal with changing perceptions of university campus functions in the era of massive open online courses (MOOCs). Each of these campuses was dimly resonant with the campus ideas of previous generations. The designs all unearth ways for these campuses to be – as Louis Kahn might have put it – what they want to be, not in the past but in the changing circumstances of the present. The designs grow out of archaeologies of sites and ideas, and they take poetic positions in relation to a range of civic ideals.

Shrine to Confucius,
Hanoi, 1070
This shrine sits in the Temple of Literature, claimed to be the oldest university in South East Asia.

Here are three instances from this century in which universities have healed themselves and their relationship to their cities. In each case a single insight into the fundamental poetic organisation of a campus gives rise to cascades of

other insights. Nothing physical changes through that high-order or 'meta' insight, and yet everything is different after it has been absorbed. Universities, like religious institutions, have always used architecture to express their missions and house their activities. Somehow their buildings and their campuses usually have a human, graspable scale. This is also true of temples and cathedrals, however large. Think of the Parthenon in Athens, or of Chartres Cathedral – their immensity is built up of components that we read in human-scale measures. We stand in Chartres and, in a personalising trick of the imagination, consider ourselves in the much more intimate scale of Paris's Sainte-Chapelle. It could be said that the pursuit of knowledge in our universities begins with the pursuit of infinity, a search that was at first a religious quest. And we find that ancient universities, whether in Hanoi or in Cambridge, expressing ideas of infinity have mathematically precise places of worship at their core.

Nicholas Close, King's College Chapel, University of Cambridge, 1441–1515 Chapels are at the core of university life in the colleges of the oldest universities.

While the majority of what is built today is erected mindlessly in the train of global capital, most universities are islands of architectural endeavour, seeking ways to express and to house their current understandings of their missions.

To do this, even universities a few generations old have to contend with layers of ambitions laid down in the past. In building for current visions of learning, they risk trampling on the poetics associated with past ideas about what universities do. We love campuses because they are palimpsests revealing the past, showing in a living archaeology the ideas for which our forebears fought. These ideas are almost always, at least in the Western tradition (China has a very different history), also about the city and how it should be reformed.[9] Each of the university makeovers presented here has its own history to contend with, and they all involve architects working with the poetics of past generations while seeking out poetics that deal with contemporary concerns.

The first of these university stories, implemented in the first decade of the 21st century, is the story of the Hargreaves Associates plan for the University of Cincinnati.[10] Without the key poetic insight that George Hargreaves and Mary Margaret Jones brought to the campus, nothing unusual would have followed. And this is a very unusual makeover. The University of Cincinnati is a State University first established in the 19th century. It occupies two square-mile (1.6-kilometre-square) blocks north of the city, a chequerboard configuration in which the blocks touch at their northeast and southwest corners while being linked into an 'L' shape by a park. The grid they occupy marches across the terrain with an abstract disdain: this is the rationalist grid of the Age of Enlightenment in which the United States was founded, and this is the grid that opened up the west. So at the outset the university boundary is ideologically charged. Axially arranged neoclassicism was the architecture of rationalism, and the first university buildings occupied the higher ground to the southwest of the southern block, a long arcing crescent giving the proper axial arrival at the portico of the main building, and other buildings making as best an axial relationship to this as the ridge would allow. Each building asserted its axial symmetry, but there was no Thomas Jefferson here to link them into a higher-order figure like that he used to lay out the University of Virginia in the years around 1820. Maybe the terrain thwarted such thinking. These square miles were grooved into flat-bottomed valleys with steep sides by the actions of glaciers in the last ice age, and from the southwest to the northeast along the diagonal of the southern block, a river used to flow. At the head of this valley the university sited its main sports

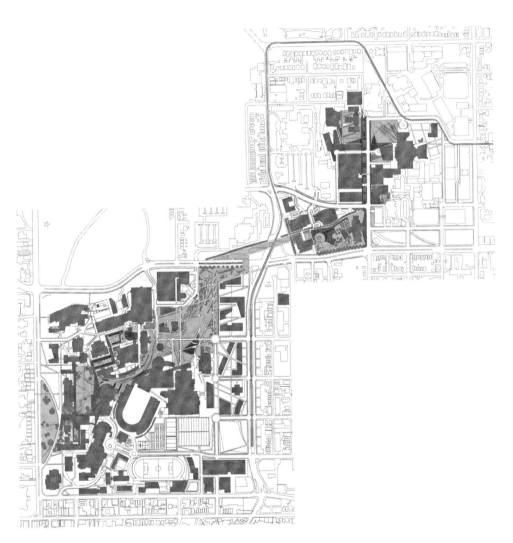

field with a horseshoe grandstand running along the flanks of the valley – a sweet and economical topographical match. Later developments in the 1970s were in the main bravely innovative structures, each asserting its own independent genius, sited in a salt-and-pepper scatter around the earlier neoclassical buildings. Some construction ideas failed and buildings were removed; others have been remediated. In the late 20th century, following the success of commissioning an architecture school – the Aronoff Center

Hargreaves Associates, University of Cincinnati Masterplan 2000, Cincinnati, Ohio, 2000
Diagram showing how the topography is used to link the two campus areas at their diagonally adjacent corners.

Hargreaves Associates,
University of Cincinnati
Masterplan 2000,
Cincinnati, Ohio, 2000
Diagram showing the ridges
and valleys of the glaciated
topography.

for Design and Art – through a limited competition won by Peter Eisenman (1996), the university was persuaded that good design could further its developmental aims. Understanding that the campus lacked a sense of place, and after reviewing many examples of university masterplans, the president and chief financial officer decided that only topographical thinking could deliver a plan for the refreshment of the campus, and they commissioned landscape architects Hargreaves Associates.

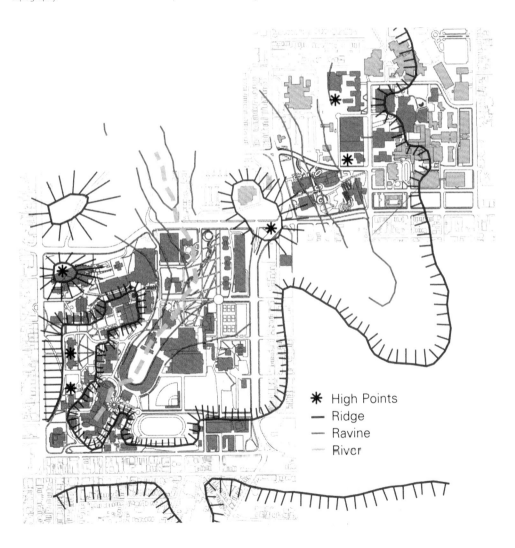

* High Points
— Ridge
— Ravine
— River

Hargreaves, in an all-changing poetic insight, rendered the topography of the campus visible, showing how the ridges fingered into the southern block and hugged the northern one, and showing how the old river flowed diagonally across the southern one and exited into the park block. Topographical thinking led to strategies that eventually gave rise to the architectural coherence of a city in miniature, structured around a civic street and having that icon of the North American city, a central park.

A number of poetic layers are at work here. The first of these is the Age of Enlightenment square-mile grid enshrining principles of egality derived from the French Revolution and given an architectural and libertarian cast by Frank Lloyd Wright in his Broadacre City project, first presented in his book *The Disappearing City* (1932).[11] The design reinforces these edges with planting. It also reveals how a tunnel under a high island at the juncture of the two square campus sites could take the traffic of the major roads that line the edges of the squares and separate them.

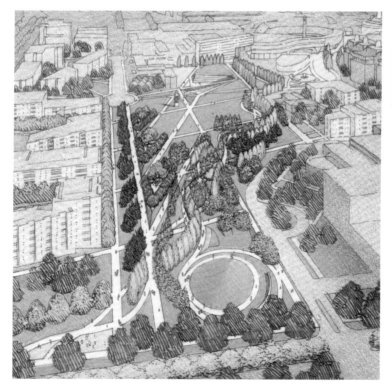

Hargreaves Associates, University of Cincinnati Masterplan 2000, Cincinnati, Ohio, 2000
View of the proposed and implemented Campus Green, as seen from above the junction with the northern campus area.

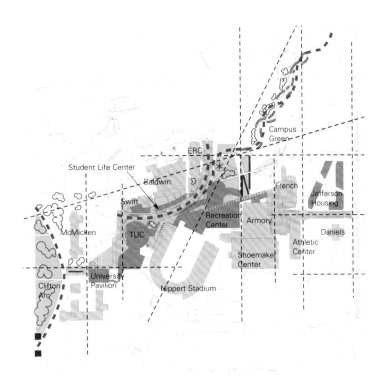

Hargreaves Associates,
University of Cincinnati
Masterplan 2000,
Cincinnati, Ohio, 2000
Plan of the Main Street
District.

The second poetic layer is the rationalist and humanitarian architecture of neoclassicism, mimicking the taxonomic impulse of the age of the encyclopedia by giving each university function and discipline its own separate building, humanising this through the architectural language of the orders – Doric and Ionic. The design locates new courtyards axially related to these buildings.

The third layer is the technical experimentation of post–Second World War optimism, but still adhering to taxonomic clarity between disciplines. The design accommodates the surviving icons from this era as follies in a flowing landscape. A new mound made of demolished material was sited to match the natural island of high ground between the two blocks and mask the traffic until such time as it was tunnelled. This mound also made a gateway to the remnant vegetation in the park, itself a square-mile block.

The fourth poetic layer is the growth of competition between universities and a post-modern relaxation of boundaries between disciplines, giving rise

Bernard Tschumi
Architects with
Glaserworks, Richard E
Lindner Varsity Village,
University of Cincinnati,
Ohio, 2006

to a desire to make physical the newly apparent flows between knowledge
areas and to create a place that can hold together this newly labile intellectual
exchange. The design creates a series of organic, off-axis connections. The
Tangeman University Center, a student centre designed by Gwathmey Siegel
(2004), assumes the quasi-platonic rationalist form of a cylinder, mediating
between the neoclassical axiality of the main building and the off-axis flow
of the new student street. The Moore Ruble Yudell-designed Joseph A Steger
Student Life Center (2004) gives a continuous, actively populated edge to
the street, housing many smaller functions. These are divided by portals
to alleys between the neoclassical buildings on top of the ridge behind,
forming spaces with steps and alcoves and walled gardens as they rise up
the ridge. The street provides a new privileged overview of the sports field
with its horseshoe amphitheatre Nippert Stadium, making its activity party
to the life of the street; this picturesque strategy creates a journey from
the formal headquarters of the university along the new student street to
a meandering park. The Recreation Centre, designed by Thom Mayne of
Morphosis Architects (2006), catches the street and deflects it on into the
new parkland, but also continues it internally as a bridge between gyms
and across an Olympic-sized swimming pool below on the bottom of the
river valley – itself an inspired poetic location – and carries it on to the other

academic buildings beyond. The university required the architects of the new buildings along the street to work together, synchronising levels, relationships of mass and materials. The result is a unifying matrix of architectural detailing and materials that forms a setting to the colourful pre-existing grandstands and places all emphasis on the activity on the street. For the very different Richard E Lindner Varsity Village, which includes an institute of sport built a little later than the street (2006), Bernard Tschumi persuaded the university to allow him to insert the building on a curved slither of land between the

O'Donnell + Tuomey, Central European University Competition, Budapest, 2011
Rendered view into one of the new courtyards.

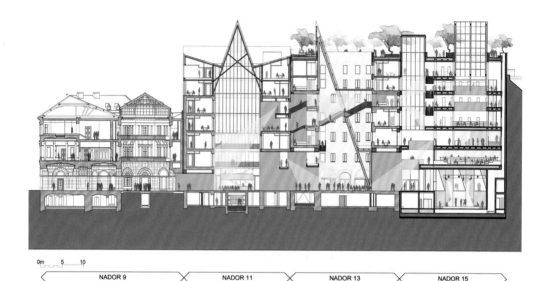

| NADOR 9 | NADOR 11 | NADOR 13 | NADOR 15 |

stadium and the rear of the recreation center – a very constrained site – and he designed a white slippery round-edged form with a slim internal crevasse-like atrium that presents a memory of a glacier sliding along its valley.

Thus the university came to understand and visualise its topography. Then it applied the city ideals of a civic spine and picturesque central park onto its neoclassical and individualist 1970s morphology. None of this now apparent 'being what it always wanted to be' could have happened without Hargreaves revealing the innate poetics of the landscape. From that central insight cascades both design and social performance: the works transformed the university's ability to attract and retain students and staff.

In 2011 architects O'Donnell + Tuomey won a competition to re-engineer the Central European University in Budapest. This involved some 30,000 square metres (320,000 square feet) of existing buildings and courtyards, two new buildings and courtyards and a new route through the university's five adjacent but separate buildings. These buildings are in the heart of the city, between an axis from the Basilica of St Stephen to the river and an offset axis back into the city grid across the face of the Hungarian Academy of Sciences at right angles to the riverbank. The urban form is a perimeter block around courtyards. Riding over this unremarkable Central European urban form are layers of institutional ambition. The city was part of the Holy Roman Empire

O'Donnell + Tuomey,
Central European
University Competition,
Budapest, 2011
Cross section showing the
atrium courtyards and the
bridges across them.

(dissolved in 1806). It was partner to Vienna in the equally multicultural Austro-Hungarian Empire (1867–1918). Prague to the north was another partner, Ljubljana to the south a junior. These were empires held together by ideas, not by national boundaries, and great thinking flowed. As nationalism began to undermine the empire, Robert Musil (1880–1942) wrote his modern epic *The Man Without Qualities*.[12] In this Diotima, a principal character, traverses the territories seeking an idea that will hold all together. In the 21st century, philanthropist George Soros is such a character, formulating and expounding ideas that may keep the body politic of Europe in balance. Education is his passion, and here as elsewhere he sponsors the developing educational programme of the university.

This Central Europe is the terrain in which Camillo Sitte (1843–1903) analysed urban form, revealing the organic syncopation of all of the most loved squares in the cities, and here he railed against the numbing abstraction of Beaux-Arts axial and symmetrical city design.[13] And from Prague to Ljubljana worked Jože Plečnik (1872–1957), that master of tweaking levels, enclosing courts and bridging rivers so that cities effortlessly look and work as they seemingly must always have 'wanted to'.[14] And

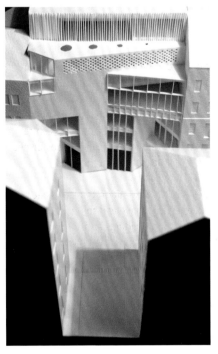

O'Donnell + Tuomey, Central European University Competition, Budapest, 2011
Model of the new facade to the south facing an axis to the river.

here in Budapest O'Donnell + Tuomey arrive to implement in this old carcass the advanced educational programmes of the contemporary university, a project less about timetabling than ever before, more about providing locales in which learners – progressing through courses in their own ways and at their own pace, drawing on the worldwide resources made available on the internet – can gather with their peers (and sometimes their mentors) to find a common sense of purpose.

The O'Donnell + Tuomey poetic insight here is that of urban dentistry: cut away the decay, remove the bad fillings (some

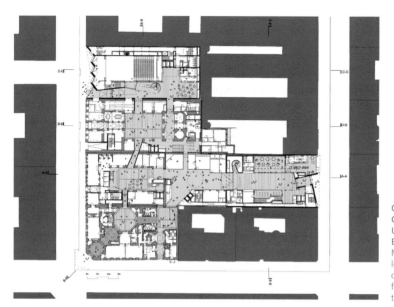

O'Donnell + Tuomey,
Central European
University Competition,
Budapest, 2011
Masterplan at street
level showing the new
connections between the
five university buildings and
the new and old courtyards.

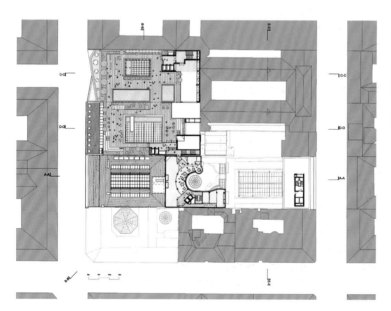

O'Donnell + Tuomey,
Central European
University Competition,
Budapest, 2011
Masterplan roofscape
showing three university
buildings fronting the street
to the left, one on the corner
and one fronting the street
to the right.

low-quality infill from the latter half of the 20th century), create a denture (that new route) that feels smooth in the mouth, and make two new insertions (with courtyards). The cutting away reveals where the opportunities for new congregative space lie, courtyards are roofed over, bridged at upper levels, and as in the prevailing urban form the new buildings have courtyards. Further respecting the historic layering, the new route through the five sites mimics the implied dogleg between the two competing existing axes. One internal arm runs parallel to the axis from the Basilica of St Stephen to the river, turns at right angles and then emerges through a new building with its new facade heading along the axis down to the river past the Hungarian Academy of Sciences on the riverbank. Thus, in the new university design, the new route through the five adjacent sites links the buildings – old and new – and echoes in miniature the larger city. O'Donnell + Tuomey's key poetic insight respects and enhances the intellectual history of the region, adds to its meaning, and structures the refreshed university around an eidetic replication of the urban structure.

In 2011, RMIT, a university of technology and design situated mainly in the northern quarter of the central business district of Melbourne, prepared a brief for adding some 5,000 square metres (50,000 square feet) of space and re-engineering around 20,000 square metres (200,000 square feet) of a block of four 12-storey buildings facing onto the civic spine of the city, and on the other side onto the central open-space spine of the campus. Expressions of interest were called for, a shortlist of five was drawn up and, from examination of the design approaches proffered, a team of five architectural practices – Harrison and White, Maddison Architects, Minifie van Schaik Architects (MvS) and NMBW Architecture Studio, led by Lyons – was selected. Design commenced in 2012. The rationale for the development was the recasting of the role played by university facilities in an age of MOOCs. For a while in the 1990s, many in university administration believed that the need for built facilities would shrink dramatically as online learning replaced face-to-face learning. The need for a place of learning would fade. The decade of investment in its campuses by RMIT in response to student complaints that (to paraphrase Gertrude Stein) 'there was no there there' was assumed to be over.[15] The emphasis, it was believed, should be on the capturing of and capitalising on a university's courseware. Then in 2002 Massachusetts Institute of Technology (MIT) put all its courseware online with unrestricted access. Understanding the implications of this – that what universities offer is high-quality space and the opportunity for face-to-face interactions – Margaret Gardner, a visionary vice chancellor at RMIT, reversed the trends of the decade and invested in a new academic building consisting largely of student portals:

Lyons, Swanston
Academic Building, RMIT
Melbourne, 2012
Unprogrammed 'Student
Portal'.

un-timetabled double-volume spaces with partly landscaped balconies,
serviced with high-speed internet connection and coffee kiosks. These reach
80 per cent occupancy levels, unprecedented in a sector in which occupancy
rates are at 20 per cent or less. Building on this success the vice chancellor,
fully realising the significance of the popularity of the Lyons-designed

THE ROSE SERIES P.2653 SWANSTON STREET. & M. U. BUILDING, MELBOURNE.
COPYRIGHT.

Marcus R Barlow,
Manchester Unity
Building, Melbourne, 1932
This terracotta-clad
skyscraper was the last of a
series of buildings aspiring to
compete with skyscrapers in
Chicago.

Swanston Academic Building (2012) for the university's ability to attract students, looked to the next step. This involved reconceiving the library and student services of the campus, largely spread along levels four and five of the large polytechnic block, and re-engineering the buildings that they occupied.

The pre-existing poetics of three of the blocks is formidable. Although situated on Swanston Street, the civic spine of the city, between the City Baths (1904) and the State Library (1854), these grey concrete structures turned their backs to the street, their 'ground' level being predicated on that of the central spine of the campus and thus half a level up from Swanston Street. For decades this had seemed simply perverse, or an accident. Maybe the 'E' of the blocks was meant to have its fingers facing Swanston Street, and a fortress mentality reversed this?

The poetic insight that changed the thinking of the team of architects emerged from a meticulous archaeological investigation into the original intentions of the building. Only the left-hand 'E' was completed. Clearly its materials and stripped-back forms were dimly resonant of numerous polytechnic buildings designed and built in the 1960s and 1970s. In its implied endlessness it owed something perhaps to Candilis, Josic, and Woods's competition design for the Free University of Berlin (1963). Drawings were unearthed that showed that the service road running beneath the blocks parallel to Swanston Street, midway up the fingers, had its origins in a service tunnel projected to run all the way down the civic spine, past the Library, the Women's Hospital (now demolished), the Town Hall and St Paul's Cathedral to the railway on the riverbank. Slab blocks, like the fingers of the RMIT building, were drawn marching at right angles to the river all the way down the spine, in the manner of Ludwig Hilberseimer (1885–1967), an architect who proposed remorselessly orthogonal city masterplans. A very real threat to the existing city fabric was more than implied. This of course owed its genesis to the idea of separating vehicular and pedestrian traffic enshrined in the 1963 Buchanan Report *Traffic in Towns*,[16] as well as to various prior musings of CIAM members from Le Corbusier to Peter and Alison Smithson. Australia, settled after the Enlightenment, thus

Bates, Smart & McCutcheon, RMIT Building 10, Melbourne, 1966
The open podium overlooking the civic spine was later closed in.

not much involved with Romanticism, and formed in the age of Benthamite utilitarianism (Jeremy Bentham's late 18th-century panopticon designs

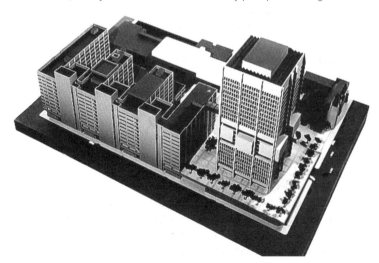

Bates, Smart & McCutcheon, completion proposal for RMIT city block, Melbourne, 1967
Only the 'E' to the left was built, adjoining Building 10 and in the same style.

Minifie van Schaik
Architects, RMIT New
Academic Street,
Melbourne, 2014
View from the street level of
the civic spine, showing the
proposed access up into the
buildings.

being implemented in prisons), was perhaps especially susceptible to such instrumental thinking. Melbourne, a city that in the 19th century competed with Chicago for the crown of having the tallest building, was perhaps particularly susceptible to these ideas, given Chicago's re-engineering of its ground plane well above natural ground level. However, late in the 19th century the money ran out, and only fragments of these grandiose city reforms were realised, here at RMIT and in one unloved and now demolished slab at right angles along the railway tracks at the other end of the spine.

What the architects were able to acknowledge, and the poetic insight from which their several design moves stemmed, was that all was not as bleak as it seemed; there was an architectural ideal lurking within the form. The half-level up was shown to have offered the potential for a privileged overview gallery to the civic spine. The circulation cores of the buildings were so situated that lanes could be cut up into the building and across to the central spine of the campus. A 'New Academic Street', as the project became known, could be driven along parallel to Swanston Street, creating a legible city grid within the blocks. The diagonally offset structure at the base of the fourth building could be used to house a broad staircase leading from the street to the heart of the new combined Library and Student Services 'street'.

Flowing from this poetic insight, there are new interior halls chiefly by Lyons, and new infill buildings in the courtyards in the 'E' by Lyons, MvS, Harrison and White and NMBW. The new configuration of the whole complex now opens to the civic spine of Swanston Street with bays by MvS and NMBW, a new corner by Harrison and White and new retail outlets by Maddison to the side opposite the historic city baths.

Lyons with NMBW Architecture Studio, Minifie van Schaik Architects, Harrison and White, and Maddison Architects, RMIT New Academic Street, Melbourne, 2014
View of the inner campus changes proposed, with a pavilion by NMBW to the left, infill building by Lyons, balcony building by Harrison and White and an infill building by Minifie van Schaik to the right.

Companion to the three university makeovers: Grafton Architects, School of Economics, Luigi Bocconi University, Milan, Italy, 2008
Situated in an existing street, the building takes its overall scale from the existing fabric, but then, using elongated light cones and clerestory glazing, opens up the basement as the populated focus of the School.

References

1. This account is adapted from: Leon van Schaik, 'Marysville 16 Hour Police Station', *Architecture Australia*, July/August 2014, pp 92–8.
2. Denise Scott Brown and Robert Venturi, *Learning from Las Vegas*, The MIT Press (Cambridge, MA), 1972; this was the first book to study signage as a possible source for architectural design.
3. See Beatriz Colomina, 'Intimacy and Spectacle: The Interiors of Adolf Loos', in John Whiteman, Jeffrey Kipnis and Richard Burdett (eds), *Strategies in Architectural Thinking*, The MIT Press (Cambridge, MA), 1992, pp 68–89.
4. In conversation on site with the author, April 2014.
5. See Andrei Voznesensky, *Antiworlds: Poems*, Oxford University Press (London), 1967.
6. See James Joyce, *Ulysses* [1922], Wordsworth Editions (Ware, Hertfordshire), 2010.
7. See Clifford Geertz, *The Interpretation of Culture*, Basic Books (New York), 1973, p 5.
8. See Colin Rowe and Fred Koetter, *Collage City*, The MIT Press (Cambridge, MA and London), 1978.
9. See Li Shiqiao, *Understanding the Chinese City*, Sage (London), 2014.
10. Unlike all the other case studies in this book, the University of Cincinnati information is derived from earlier research – specifically for Leon van Schaik and Geoffrey London, *Procuring Innovative Architecture*, Routledge (London), 2010 – and did not involve the usual process of discussion of the ideogram.
11. Frank Lloyd Wright, *The Disappearing City*, WF Payson (New York), 1932.
12. Robert Musil, *The Man Without Qualities* [*Der Mann ohne Eigenschaften*, 1940], translated by Sophie Wilkins, Picador (London), 1995.
13. See George R Collins and Christiane C Collins, *Camillo Sitte: The Birth of Modern City Planning*, Rizzoli (New York), 1986.
14. See Peter Krečič, *Plečnik: The Complete Works*, Whitney Library of Design (New York), 1993.
15. Stein wrote of Oakland, California: 'there is no there there': Gertrude Stein, *Everybody's Autobiography*, Random House (New York), p 289.
16. Colin Buchanan, *The Buchanan Report: Traffic in Towns*, HMSO (London), 1963, and *Traffic in Towns: The Specially Shortened Edition of the Buchanan Report S228*, Penguin Books (Harmondsworth), 1964.

Capturing Nature

4

In the Anthropocene, architecture turns to capturing nature. At various scales, the projects in these case studies seek to put people in the position of being in a natural context. Here they will be intensely aware of the passage of light, of navigating through ravines and up escarpments, of following undulating hills, of inhabiting a coastal area and of living in a forest. Within a generation, 75 per cent of the world's population will live in cities. Architecture paradoxically will provide them with most of their experiences of the wild, the seemingly un-made. These case studies reveal this new poetics in the early stages of its manifestation.

Kristen Green
Architecture, La Plage,
Vanuatu, ongoing

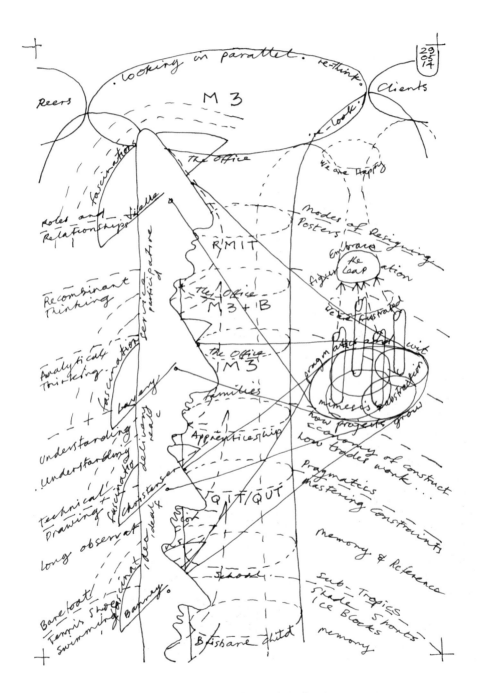

University of Queensland Aquatic Centre, Brisbane

m3architecture, 2012

m3architecture is a partnership in Brisbane which, through a period of reflective research, has encapsulated 15 poetic thresholds that their practice uses. In the process they analysed their roles and relationships, their shared experiences of childhood and of apprenticeship. Their poetics captures nature but is far from romantic; rather, it is pragmatic.

Nearly ten years ago, when I was writing *Mastering Architecture* and thinking through for the first time the relationships between our own research into creative practice and that of Howard Gardner and Randall Collins,[1] and realising that the tri-polarity that Collins had discovered underpinned periods of intellectual change that had already been identified two thousand years earlier by Vitruvius, my RMIT colleague Martyn Hook pointed out that many ambitious younger practices had formed out of alliances between three people. His own practice – their research into their designing processes indicated – had a dynamic between a practice caretaker for poetics, a caretaker for pragmatics and one for social sustainability.[2]

m3architecture started as such a triad. Three Michaels with three different focuses met at college.[3] On the face of it, Michael Banney covered issues of social and cultural engagement, Michael Christensen embraced technical pragmatics and Michael Lavery offered a direct take on poetics. Research into the nature of tri-polarity in ambitious architectural practice has revealed a more and more modulated spectrum of triangulations,[4] and even with the qualifier that all three Michaels work in all three identified spheres, we would not today leave anyone so labelled. This is fortunate because Ben Vielle joined the three Michaels, so even numerically the practice defies such labelling. The four principals have to an unusual extent woven a design practice that has a single voice. This, through the agency of a few small projects, is the focus of this case study. Some context is needed, for the conditions within which practices operate are different to those in Europe, North America and Japan. m3architecture practise in a rich country in GDP terms, but that wealth is spread very thinly across a vast continent with a small population, 80 per cent of which has for over a hundred years lived in six coastal cities, capitals each of their respective States in the Commonwealth of Australia. Distance inflates infrastructure costs, and most building projects are undertaken with a fraction of the money devoted to similar projects elsewhere. A very particular kind of ingenuity operates in the good architecture of the country. An example of this in the work of m3architecture is the motorway-facing wall of the Learning Centre of Brisbane Girls Grammar School (2007), where a simple pattern of paint on the wall and a sun screen of black battens standing a metre (3 feet) away create a rolling moiré effect that registers at the scale of the highway. It returns great impact for very little outlay.

m3architecture, University of Queensland Aquatic Centre – David Theile Olympic Pool, Brisbane, 2012
General view from outside the complex. Note the blue reflected on the gloss squares painted on the soffit of the roof.

m3architecture have studied the way in which they work exhaustively.[5] They understand that they share spatial histories common to most people who have had a childhood and schooling in the sub-tropics of suburban Brisbane, and they share a common route to professional life through their architectural education. Their own young families are going through the same childhood experiences, lives focused on swimming pools, shade seeking, sand shoe wearing, sucking 'ice-blocks' (the local name for sorbets) … Knowing the differences between themselves, they have built up a process of 'parallel looking' in which at the concept stage of projects they bring all their intelligences to bear. They have completed numerous projects at many scales, the larger ones being additions to schools, research institutes and university departments, the smaller ones including sports pavilions, memorials and temporary settings for large functions. They have also refurbished a found building to suit the flat hierarchy of their practice.

Of these, their University of Queensland Aquatic Centre and David Theile Olympic Pool (2012) has an intense poetic impact on me, perhaps because I too had a childhood in which swimming loomed large. All m3architecture projects have this intensity, often delivered through a surprising twist. The University's sports fields are spread along the flood plane of a river that curves around the headland on which the acropolis of the university sits. In 2011 the pool, changing rooms and all of the equipment were inundated in an exceptionally extreme flood, after which all that was still

m3architecture, University of Queensland Aquatic Centre – David Theile Olympic Pool, Brisbane, 2012
Even casual passers-by have their attention captured by the effect of the pool reflected upwards – it is as if they were looking at the surface of water from below.

fit for use were the shells of the pools and the berms formed when they were excavated some forty years earlier. Suddenly, rebuilding became an imperative – not simply for the university but also for the schools and inhabitants of the western suburbs who relied on the pool. While the old changing rooms were very utilitarian – blockwork walls and a tin roof – the site held summer memories for everyone in the area. The economics forced the retention of the pool shells, and m3architecture's understanding of how the local construction industry works forged a design based on sequencing the trades, which rapidly brought into existence a large planar roof supported on 4.5-metre- (15-foot-) high columns. This roof provided far more shade for the pool than the original shelter, and it also allowed the later construction of the walls of changing rooms, plant rooms, learning spaces and a café. The columns are painted 'River Brown' up to the datum of the flood, white above, and the ceiling is a white plane. In future floods, the roof is designed to remain in place. The berms have been reinforced and their amphitheatre and lounging functions have been extended. At the entrance a handrail leads you in, jumping to the flood datum level as it ends at the ticket kiosk. Contemporary privacy concerns (which also govern the

m3architecture with Brian Hooper Architect, Barcaldine Tree of Knowledge, Barcaldine, Queensland, 2009
The hanging timber slats define the space formerly occupied by the tree canopy.

design of the changing rooms) mean that the pool is almost invisible from outside its boundary fence.

The architects were vividly aware of the phenomenon of glimpsing – from the acropolis – the water surface reflecting the sky at dawn when the first swimming classes commence, and at sunset, when they used to end. Together they studied the visibility problem. Michael Lavery envisaged the way in which when you are underwater the surface of the water becomes seemingly separate from the water itself. How, they wondered, could this be delivered by the underside of the large floating shade roof? Already at some sun angles, ripples in the pool bounced light up onto it. And at other angles the whole ceiling was suffused with the soft blue of the pool itself. They hit upon the idea of painting a grid of gloss squares onto the matt surface of the ceiling. This now, as you walk by, catches your peripheral vision with strong reflections from the surface of the pool. It is indeed rather like looking up into that water skin from deep in the pool. Very simply, an eidetic community poetics is captured and enhanced. This architectural intelligence is akin to theatrical Ars Povera: maximum effect through minimal but clever use of resources at hand.

m3architecture,
preparatory image for the
Yeerongpilly Footbridge,
Brisbane, 2010
The sole of a Dunlop Volley
tennis shoe is transected by
the pattern for the bridge.

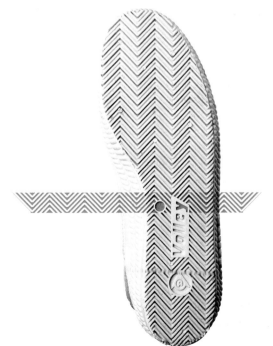

That this is not an accident but a deliberate strategy is demonstrated in each of the practice's projects. Their Barcaldine Tree Of Knowledge (2009), a memorial to the tree under which the Australian Labor Party was founded, places a box of strips of timbers over the site of the poisoned tree. Hanging down at different lengths, these create the negative space of the canopy that once existed. From the street you see an impressive if enigmatic timber slatted box raised up above head height. Walk under and you are flipped into wonder with the same eidetic force that the reflections at the pool produce. Gaston Bachelard would say, I imagine, that you are flipped into reverie, as you are when reading a great line in a poem.[6]

m3architecture model their process as the four overlapping investigations of their concerns for pragmatics (always a key for them), their analytical and abstracting thinking, their belief in processes that mesh every intelligence (in the office, in their clients and in their consultants) and an acceptance that there will be a period of frustration in which none of them is happy with the figuration of the design. Then, through their 'parallel looking', they all contribute ideas that might unlock the potential they have created, and then in the conversation one idea emerges and is accepted as the most

m3architecture,
Yeerongpilly Footbridge,
Brisbane, 2010
The sole pattern as applied
to the bridge.

potent, and they act. In a series of posters, they have captured the kinds of moves that work – the engines of the wit that unlocks designs for them.

One of these concerns the Yeerongpilly Footbridge (2010). The practice was commissioned to rework a bridge linking – across a main road – a train station to a nearby major tennis venue. A standard Warren truss had been selected, and this was considered economical but lacking in charisma. In their usual process, m3architecture wrestled with this, coming up with bouncing ball motifs – anything to disguise the crude frame of the bridge. Then they embraced the pragmatics of the truss, and floating into mind came the zigzag tread of professional tennis shoes of yesteryear and now the retro footwear every child in their city wears. The well-remembered sole pattern fitted the triangulations of the bridge, and suddenly they had the fit to the structure and to the poetics that they were seeking. These tennis shoes have carried generations into spatial awareness, and now they signal the unlikely spatial connection between a train station on one side of a busy road and the tennis centre on the other.

The work of m3architecture, at every scale, is replete with such moments of delight, the result of the intense and consciously mastered poetic insights of the group.

Companion to University of Queensland Aquatic Centre: SANAA (Kazuyo Sejima and Ryue Nishizawa), Serpentine Gallery Pavilion, London, 2009
This lightweight pavilion with its highly reflective ceiling sucked the canopies of the surrounding trees down into its interior.

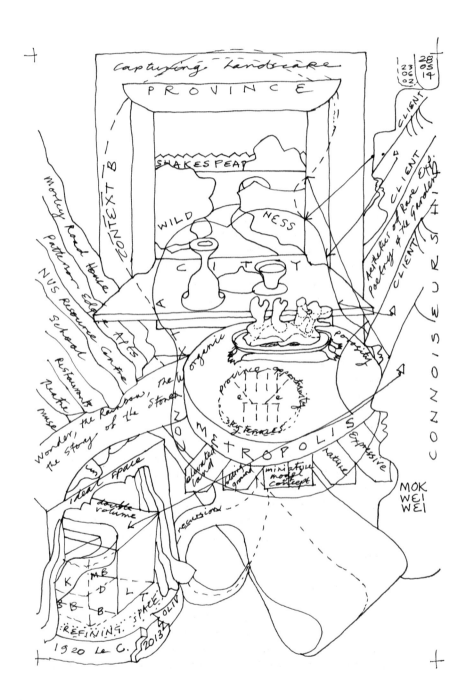

Capturing Landscape

PROVINCE

SHAKESPEA?

WILD   NESS

CONTEXT B

CLIENT
CLIENT
Aesthetics of Rare City
Poetry of the Gardens
CLIENT
CLIENTS #

Money Road House
Patterson Edge Apts
NUS Resource Centre
School
Restaurant
Theatre
Museum

Wonder, the Rainbow,
the Story of the Stone

the organic

potential

province opportunity

METROPOLIS

SKY TERRACES

CONNOISEURS #

expressive

nature

MOK
WEI
WEI

ideal space

double
volume

curated
land

cultured
ground

miniature
model
concept

recursion

K   MB
D'   L
B   B
S B   B   T
SPACE   OLIV
REFINING   2013

1920 Le C.

28
05
14
23
06
02

The Oliv, Singapore

W Architects, 2013

W Architects is an award-winning practice in Singapore. It has represented Singapore at the Venice Biennale, and grew out of the partnership between Mok Wei Wei and veteran architect and urban theorist William Lim. The poetics of the practice is post-colonial in that every design reveals the role of cultural memories in the mental space of architects, connoisseurs, and the increasing number of bicultural people in the world.

We are social beings, very much formed by our relationships with our families and our friends in fairly well-documented rings of contact, family (half of whom may be adversaries) and close friendships forged through periods of intellectual awakening, 'relationships that you pick up where you left off even after decades' to the fore.[7] You might think this would isolate us in friendly ghettos. Yet, while teenagers are profoundly influenced by their peers in seemingly homogeneous groups, more and more of us – inhabiting a post-colonial or late imperial world – grow up straddling cultures. We owe allegiance to the art, literature, music and architecture of more than one tradition. This has a profound impact on how our poetics are formed and how they play out in designing. The same thing in one context may be provincial, in another metropolitan.

Those who inhabit psycho-islands formed by Chinese diasporas within former British colonies negotiate a particularly rich mixture of traditions.[8] For older people in these states there are memories of being discriminated against or, worse still, of being patronised. For younger people there is a strange seesawing between metropolitan and provincial conditions, with no certain formula for determining what part of an experience will be cosmopolitan, what part parochial. Where the English language has mostly supplanted the Chinese, this is particularly fraught. Shakespeare is in mind, in his native tongue, yet we read *The Story of the Stone*, the 18th-century Chinese epic, in translation in the Penguin Classics.[9] All sorts of unlikely tendrils of culture mix in unpredictable ways. Architecture is similarly conflicted. As there is no such thing as space until it is observed, the observing of it colours it completely. Mok Wei Wei, the subject of this case study, had an unusual upbringing in Anglophone Singapore, where Chinese was and is taught in schools as a second language, and is not used as the medium of instruction. His father edited the sole Chinese-language newspaper in the city-state,

Leon van Schaik, research ideogram, 28 May 2014 Drawn at the conclusion of researching the project.

and Wei Wei grew up speaking Chinese and English at home and at school, but had to switch to English only at university. For citizens of Chinese origin, benefiting in a mercantile sense from the umbrella of the British rule of law, such resistance to the Anglophone culture that there was, whether one spoke English at home or not, resided in connoisseurial passions for Chinese furniture, calligraphy-inspired art, gardens and food. And while architecture was taught through what we now discern as the tri-polar modernist cannon exemplified by Le Corbusier, Mies van der Rohe and Frank Lloyd Wright, there persisted in these states an entirely different spatial consciousness stemming from the anti-axial arrangements of Chinese palace and temple complexes and Chinese gardens. This was not a counterforce in the educated elites alone; it pervaded popular culture and manifested itself in the domestic arrangements of every home.

Thus it was that when Wei Wei attracted attention for the virtuoso design of the Morley Road House (1998), a large villa, what the critics hailed was exemplary neo-modernist architecture. They were mistaken. While the subtlety and intensity of the tectonics rivalled those of European minimalists, inventing new ways of making the forms of the house ambiguous through the striation of stone, the spatial arrangements of the design were simply not modernist – they were Chinese.[10]

The Chinese diaspora invented its own building type, the 'godown' or

W Architects, The Oliv, Singapore, 2013
View of the apartment building with its sky terraces. Note how these kick up and down at the right-hand side.

shop-house, a terraced form with an internal courtyard dividing a warehouse and trading hall from domestic services behind and above. Those that survive in Singapore have been gentrified in modernist and postmodernist idioms. In a poignant exemplar highlighting this argument, Wei Wei made such a conversion for one of his peers, an internationally recognised Shakespeare scholar who had returned home to look after her widowed mother. The design (2007) refreshes the house and uses the dichotomy to create a separate area for the mother, but at the core of the new vertical integration is a Studiolo devoted to representing and studying Shakespeare.

The physical development of Malaysia, Singapore and Hong Kong is determined by highly regimented regulations stemming from the 1870s bye-laws of Birmingham in England, the pioneering urban hygiene regime that sought to deal with the excesses of the Industrial Revolution. While these are somewhat resented, they have ensured a basic standard that eludes those states that have abandoned them. Designing in Singapore, architects tread a fine line between their own and their community's cultural understanding of spatiality and a rigorous if evolving set of regulations. Every architect in Singapore spends a major part of their designing time in working out how – within the regulations – to achieve a high-quality design and a financial return for their client. Thus it was that in his award-winning Paterson Edge apartment complex (1999) – an elegant glass-fronted slab facing the immensely tall trees along one of the city's boulevards, resonating in its elegant detailing with Jean Nouvel's Fondation Cartier complex in Paris (1994) – there were no balconies. The regulations would have included the area of these in the gross floor area (GFA) of each apartment, and this made them unaffordable.

Paterson Edge in a sense 'mines' its situation, relying on the pre-existing trees to shield its glass walls from direct insolation. In this it mimics the Singapore paradigm: a city that frames an amplified and sanitised version of tropical nature within its compass. Once – even two decades ago – this seemed unusual; now, with urban living the norm for most people, the capturing and presenting of a natural experience is a design theme everywhere. Stefano Boeri's Bosco Verticale (Vertical Forest) apartments in Milan (2014) are a European example. Wei Wei's The Oliv apartments (2013) are a Singapore forerunner. Through a series of apartment buildings, the practice has been perfecting an apartment type that had a genesis in certain works by Le Corbusier, such as the studio for the artist Amédée Ozenfant in Paris (1922) and the double-volume/single-volume apartment type of the Unité d'Habitation in Marseille (1952). At The Oliv, duplexes are stacked in pairs linked by vertical circulation at the centre block, two facing the street, two the pool area to the rear. A double volume contains the living and dining area, and a kitchen faces into this with a service balcony to the rear, from which – in an echo of the shophouse – a bedroom with en-suite bathroom is reached.

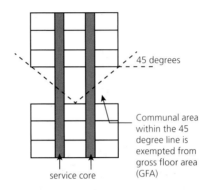

45 degrees

Communal area within the 45 degree line is exempted from gross floor area (GFA)

service core

W Architects, The Oliv, Singapore, 2013
This exemption diagram was prepared to make a case to the Urban Redevelopment Authority in Singapore. It argues that the shared external area below the dotted lines is exempt from the gross floor area calculations.

The other bedrooms are on two levels flanking the dining and living volume.

Interpreting the new regulations devised to encourage a greener city, Wei Wei realised that he could wrap a sky terrace around the building without incurring a GFA penalty if the terrace was at least putatively a common area. Given that the terrace occurred every second storey and could only ever be shared by the two apartments adjacent to it, this meant that the double volumes could face a broad deck, planted at its perimeters, and that the sky terrace above could form a glare-diffusing canopy.

To avoid possible viewing into the bedroom levels to the sides of the double volumes, Wei Wei tilted the sky terrace up at a steep angle, creating the sense of a continuous coiling from level to level up the

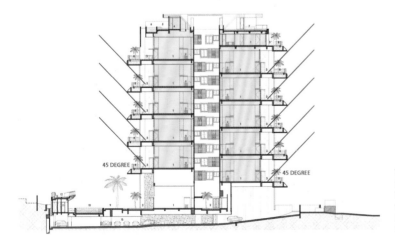

45 DEGREE   45 DEGREE

W Architects, The Oliv, Singapore, 2013
The section shows how this works in the case of The Oliv: a portion of each sky terrace is treated as a common area.

building. He used this lazy 'L' form as a miniature to house the pool room and gym, similarly to how Frank Lloyd Wright, at the Winslow House in River Forest, Illinois (1894), used a doll's-house version of the whole building to set up a reflective dialogue between inhabiting and observing the form of the house.

The warping of the timber-faced edges of the planter balustrades accentuates the sense of a coiling form rising up the building. The result is a powerful equanimity: the public life of the family takes place in the double volume, which can be viewed, theatre-like, from mezzanines on both sides, and which in turn looks out across the broad, notionally communal deck to the planted edge, and this suggests being in the forest that moderates the tropical climate of the

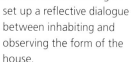

island. The bedrooms and domestic services are layered around the double volume in successive levels of privacy, a spatial arrangement reminiscent of the many thresholds of Chinese palace compounds.

W Architects, The Oliv, Singapore, 2013
A fragment of the twisting timber-clad sky terrace is used to make the roof and roof deck over the pool room and gym.

Ancient labyrinth and modern rational double volume coexist, and this forces a reading that is provincial and modern by turns, depending on whether you look at it through the lens of modern architecture or the lens of the Chinese tradition. Either way, the lesson of *The Story of the Stone* is manifest: this is an architecture that builds on what exists, and adds a new formulation and new insight to what is or ought to be well known.

Companion to The Oliv, Singapore: Stefano Boeri, rendering of Bosco Verticale, Milan, 2014
Trees grown off site during the period of construction were craned into position when the building was completed.

La Plage du Pacifique, Vanuatu

Kristin Green Architecture, ongoing

Kristin Green is a Melbourne architect whose work lies mainly in the hospitality sector. Few industries rely more on strong poetic expression. Kristin's chief client specialises in venues with individual identities that attract patronage from well-defined cultural tribes. Here Kristin's designs reveal the poetic thresholds that give the projects their niche appeal.

Most semesters Kristin Green runs a design studio at RMIT, involving a dozen students in her research into the poetics of space. Her approach has seemed visionary and idealistic, but it is now manifest in two projects, one small in scale, the other large and expansive. The smaller, the Spring Street Grocer in Melbourne (2013), is open and available for viewing as a work in its own

Kristin Green Architecture, La Plage du Pacifique, Vanuatu, ongoing
The resort is scattered across the strand, its hulks seemingly washed up and eroded into sympathy with its surroundings.

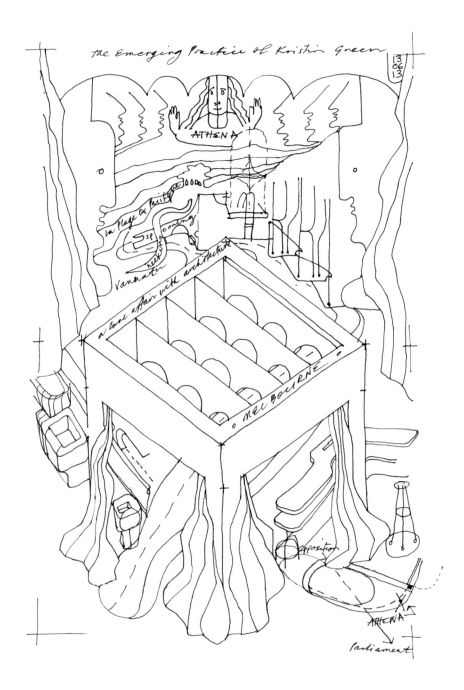

the Emerging Practice of Kristin Green

ATHENA

la Plage Du Pacifique

Vanuatu

a love affair with architecture

MELBOURNE

opposition

ATHENA

parliament

right, while the large resort, La Plage du Pacifique in Vanuatu, is still a work in progress. Both reveal the architect's maturing approach to capturing and enshrining insights into poetics of place, location and culture.

Paradoxically – given the large scale of the Vanuatu project – both projects use the same technique of close observation and direct, almost unmediated, expression. It is the almost spontaneous translation from a lyrical and inclusive appreciation into form that makes this architectural imagination present itself as a miniaturising conception. Experiencing the works, I find it hard to resist the feeling that, in both instances, I am dealing with a toy. Not a predictable mass-produced one, with wrappings that far outweigh the interest of the object itself, but a lovingly crafted, personally made gift that delights with every turn of your gaze, every touch and stroke of a surface. You can enjoy the architecture of the Spring Street Grocer as a surface-moulded space because it is composed of glazed bricks that hold the space steady in a glistening shimmer.

Kristin Green
Architecture, La Plage
du Pacifique, Vanuatu,
ongoing
The rooms host itinerant
occupation; raw materials
are softened by rugs and
flowers.

Leon van Schaik, research
ideogram, 13 June 2013
Drawn at the conclusion of
researching the project.

At the resort in Vanuatu, the arched concrete surfaces are kept raw, and the architectural idea is that these present as found objects, hulks swept up on the beach and moulded by weather and by the sympathetic magic of the curling shapes of the windswept trees. The concrete caves are then inhabited with rugs and tapestries and mattresses laid on top of these. This is a holiday encampment with none of the cloying sameness of hotel bling that oozes out of almost every hotel chain across the world.

At the Spring Street Grocer – coffee stall, grocery shop and sandwich counter on the upper level, cheese room in the basement – the glazed bricks have been marshalled and combined to make the walls, alcoves, window surrounds, floor lighting ports, counters and cheese-washing basins. Inserted into the spaces on both levels are sinuously curving shelves that morph into benches, all standing *en pointe* (Green grew up with the ballet) so that the floor can be seen to flow continuously as a surface. The cheese table in the basement suggests architecture of a vastly larger scale, and rivals the painterly imagination of architect Will Alsop. But nothing is merely formal, or wilful. The table has been worked up in detailed consultation with the cheese master. It is functional, and comfortable to sit and work at. The same is true of the counters upstairs and of the swimming pool ladder between counter and kitchen. And all is cheerful!

Green's mastery of spatiality is simply demonstrated in the basement. This is a very tight space, with minimum head height, yet it feels spacious. Green has set a dado low and kept the glazed tiles away from the concrete ceiling, ending the tiling with a cornice, which conceals lights that wash up the concrete surface. Down here the chairs are lower than usual, completing the miniaturisation of the space, and provoking a Lilliputian reading of the cheese room as a large space for the small child within. The elegant spiral stair that links the two floors could have disrupted the impression of a large space, but Green has made a calligraphy of the railings (almost spelling out 'KG') and this turns it, too, into a toy of indeterminate scale.

Kristin Green Architecture, La Plage du Pacifique, Vanuatu, ongoing
Plan, section and elevation of a typical guest villa.
1 salle de bain
2 salon
3 bathing
4 boudoir
5 banquette

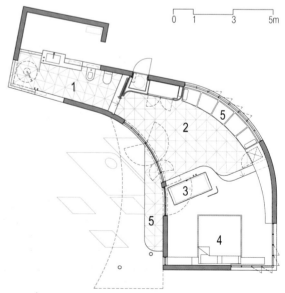

The play does not end here. Rounded door heads and window bases invert the window shapes in Parliament House across the road. We are in opposing space. The horizontal windows with curved ends slide along the outer surfaces, some projecting more than others to talk (says the architect) of the inequality of power inherent in our democracy. And upstairs on the corner entrance, steps have been scooped out to echo (in miniature) the phalanx of front steps to Parliament House.

Kristin Green
Architecture, La Plage
du Pacifique, Vanuatu,
ongoing
The hotel is conceived as an
abandoned hulk, reoccupied
by intrepid holidaymakers.

What of the resort at Vanuatu? Firstly, let me address the architectural
conception: love – *agape* – is at its core. Observing the site, Green was very
taken by the organic necking and spooning of the curves of the shoreline
in plan, and of the looping and caressing of tree trunks in the coastal
vegetation. A photograph shows a worker on site lying asleep, slumped in the
hammock shape of a tree trunk. In Green's plan, forms cup and spoon; and in
the building, walls curve, stairs take on the wind-determined buttress shapes
of tree trunks and the landing swells and spreads like the wind-trimmed
canopy of a tree, over-sailing the curving walls. Openings are scooped up
or down out of the walls, making them, too, seem to be organically arching
up from buried or lost budding points. These openings are shored up with
timber in serried 'V' mullions. They give a sense of beachcombing ingenuity,
contingent, casual and understated. Shallow contour walls inscribe high-tide
marks in sinuous counterpoint to the necking and spooning building shells.

One photograph is of a room that has been dressed by Green, a
demonstration of how to occupy the space. Here we see – in an echo of

the virtuosity of the Spring Street Grocer – floor tiling that seems artlessly, inevitably right. Highly patterned fabric covers a thick mattress on a timber bed frame; flowers, fruit and a bathing sarong lie about; and the concrete surfaces flow smoothly and continuously, the walls showing the grain of the timber shuttering.

La Plage du Pacifique is a building in the final stages of construction. In the world of luxury resorts today, the ultimate luxury lies in being able to inhabit an island that seems to be undeveloped. The discerning and unfortunately necessarily wealthy can feel as if they are Robinson Crusoe, making do and startled at just the right moment – that instant before ennui sets in – by a footprint in the sand. The poetics is that of a ruin supporting temporary occupation by these itinerants, beached here in the aftermath of a storm that has swept across it, and they and the rooms are drying out, the peace of exhaustion in the air. Knowing the Spring Street Grocer, and seeing the resort room dressed by Green, we can imagine a certain kind of completion,

Kristin Green Architecture, La Plage du Pacifique, Vanuatu, ongoing
V-shaped mullions in the openings ensure a sense of an occupation of the hulks after their construction.

and it is a compelling architectural and entrepreneurial vision. Vouching for the intentionality of the vision are the differences between this and the restaurateur Con Christopoulos's other Melbourne venues. The Neapoli wine bar (2012) is a crowded double volume with a mezzanine laden with tables for groups pressing down on the bar, and perimeter counters allowing occupation by drinkers and diners solo or duo. The compression of space at Neapoli is similar to that which artist Edward Kienholz achieved in *The Beanery* (1965; Stedelijk Museum, Amsterdam), a near life-sized walk-in representation of a Los Angeles bar. At Kirk's Wine Bar (2014) there is, in the plate-glass windows facing a tight intersection of narrow streets, the strange clarity that artist Edward Hopper sought out in his paintings, notably *Nighthawks* (1942; Art Institute of Chicago). Client and architect share what for the client is an instinct for enhancing the particularities of a venue, and what for the architect is a deliberate and deeply contemplated and reflected-upon craft of spatial thinking.

Companion to La Plage du Pacifique: Sarah Calburn, sketch design for Loop House, False Bay, South Africa (unbuilt), 2009
Sarah Calburn's project drawings always give the site an equal weight to the proposed structures.

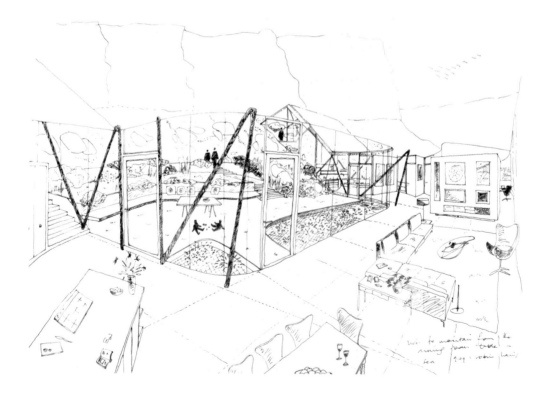

PARKROYAL on Pickering, Singapore

WOHA, 2013

WOHA is an award-winning architectural practice founded by architects Wong Mun Summ and Richard Hassell. They practise within an articulated position about working in the Anthropocene, the epoch in which human activity exerts a great force on the climate of the planet. They have developed a poetics that mines nature, abstracting form from its phenomena and thus creating built terrains.

As the giants of Asia emerge again on the world stage, with China recently becoming the world's largest economy, the way people frame their mental space changes, imperceptibly at first, and then they awake and, if they examine their thinking, find that everything is different. There are unpredictable consequences of such shifts: the acceptance that human rights extend to all members of society, not only the religious, is among these. The emergence of China and India faces us all with the fact that it is not only the resource-consuming elites of the 20th and 21st centuries who live in the Anthropocene.

The changing framing of mental space in art, media and literature is evident in Edward St Aubyn's recent novel *Lost for Words* (2014), a comedy of manners centred on a book prize for writing in the Commonwealth (a residual trace of the British Empire). The most acute lines are given to Mr Wo, a Chinese magnate who has purchased the corporation that funds the prize, and his wife. Mr Wo delivers the novel's punchline: 'Personally I think competition should be encouraged in war and sport and business, but that it makes no sense in the arts. If an artist is good, nobody else can do what he or she does, and therefore all comparisons are incoherent.'[12] Certainly no two good architectural practices create the same mental frames, but everywhere more of Asia than the 20th-century fascination with Japan is now acting on the imaginations of architects. WOHA, the practice formed by Singapore-born and -educated Wong Mun Summ and Western Australia-born and -educated Richard Hassell, gives us an indication of the riches that come from this wider embrace. WOHA practises largely in the 'exploding' cities that characterise the Anthropocene, and the firm is included here because of what their design of the hotel PARKROYAL on Pickering (2013) in Singapore says about the changing ways in which architects design for a world where, as Richard Hassell says, humans choose the forms that nature

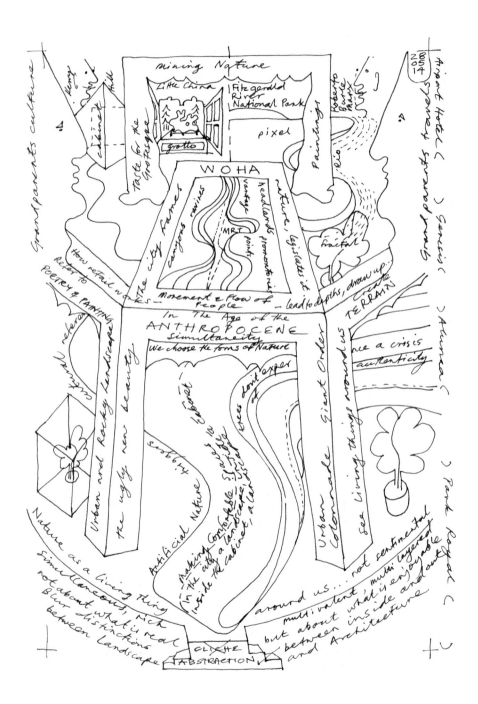

WOHA, PARKROYAL on Pickering, Singapore, 2013 Viewed from the park opposite, the contouring and planting obscure the structural grid and assert an artificial natural form.

takes. The PARKROYAL hotel and office block complex is not a new type; the same is visible in Cincinnati's French Art Deco Carew Tower and Hilton Cincinnati Netherland Plaza complex (1931), but where that signals the urban suavity of the Fred Astaire and Ginger Rogers decade, the PARKROYAL design addresses the Anthropocene by inserting amplified natural form into a mid-city block.

Rather as, in the first half of the 18th century in Bavaria, the Asam brothers affirmed Catholic mysticism through the swelling theatrical forms of Rococo, making the heavenly realm palpable above the swelling clouds of plasterwork and paint, at the PARKROYAL a block-long super-order colonnade pierces a massive contoured form that masks a five-storey podium surmounted by a garden deck. This landscape in the air is punctuated with conversation cocoons and defined by rustic rock walls and a horizon-hugging swimming pool. The tree canopies of the adjacent park are 'borrowed' as in Japanese practice, and view-lines to the city traverse nearby buildings to the city silhouette. As if through the wisps of cloud in a Baroque painting, the columns soar up through this pocket Eden to support the 'E' plan of the orthogonal hotel above, each level dripping with plants. The Anthropocene calls forth a theatrically enhanced natural scene.

Leon van Schaik, research ideogram, 28 May 2014 Drawn at the conclusion of researching the project.

What I see is an 'inverted contour' model, and I read into it natural forms such as ravines, canyons, narrow defiles, headlands and valleys. And indeed these are the words used by WOHA to describe how they were led to this kind of designing by the retail developer of their earlier Iluma project (2009), where the aim was to entice people to descend into the basement levels and up into the higher storeys. Here WOHA deploy a ceiling carving that mimics the flows of contours, an idea that emerged when they were designing the public spaces of their airport hotel, the Crowne Plaza (2008), on a site hugely compromised by the curves of existing roads, underpasses and entrances to loading docks and car parks. There it created a coherent flow between separated spaces, and at the Genexis Theatre (2008) the idea was deployed to make organic sense of a set of awkward spaces left over by other architects, the notion of contouring becoming fully three-dimensional. At Iluma the contoured ceilings echoed the creations of canyons and headland. In a later project, Wilkie Edge (2010), a scatter of cloud-shaped cut-outs in every flat soffit suggests another relationship with nature. The exterior of Iluma is covered in an organic pixelation that shocked the modernist architects in the city-state, but to WOHA they were no less engaged in abstraction than Roberto Burle Marx was in 1970 when he inscribed sine waves on the foreshore walkways of Rio de Janeiro.

WOHA, PARKROYAL on Pickering, Singapore, 2013
Viewed along the boulevard edge, the contours overhead in the colonnade claim the attention of the peripheral vision of passers-by, creating a sense of the natural rather than of the built.

The idea of 'mining nature' came to WOHA before this. When in 2000 they were designing their Metro Rail Transit stations, and wanted to avoid making boxes under the ground, they reasoned that they could work with the construction process and use a canyon form to open the stations to the sky and to natural light. Richard, inspired by childhood experiences of the landscape of the Fitzgerald River National Park in Western Australia, had been 'mining nature' through making paintings that explored its underlying fractals. He was encouraged in this by Mun Summ, with whom he had been apprenticed in the modernist practice of Kerry Hill. Mun Summ, in the spirit of

WOHA, Iluma, Singapore, 2009
The interior of this complex uses simulated headlands and contours to persuade people to visit upper and lower levels.

Mrs Wo – 'In China we put a great emphasis on naturalness, which of course can only come from the mastery of artifice'[13] – could see how his family had represented their understanding of nature through the artificial grotesqueries of a memorial grotto that graced their home, and that of every other Sinophile anywhere, including Richard's grandparents, who like mine, filled glass cabinets with porcelain figures and – if very sophisticated – knobbly rocks with a hole in them supported on a fitted mahogany tray with ball-and-claw legs

Both know, as they strive 'to make comfortable space in the city', that form always refers to the poetry and the painting of the observer's culture. In the

WOHA, Genexis Theatre,
Singapore, 2008
Contoured planes define
the foyer space surrounding
the theatre, suggesting a
landscape.

hotel, the contoured ceilings mould the spatial perceptions of visitors all the
way from the exterior through the public spaces, where bars and counters
keep the illusion going. The fifth-floor garden is a space to pause between
this kind of artifice, and it introduces another kind: that of the privileged
overview of the world beyond, a situation that humans have sought out for
millennia. In the rooms above, there is a further artifice: the bedrooms are
lined with deep cabinetry, making it feel as if you are cosseted in a large
piece of furniture, like St Jerome in his study. And in these rooms there are
supposed to be bonsai trees: the contour artifice of the podium supports
slabs of cabinet rooms that contain an artifice of the forest. Nowadays, the
city contains nature; it is not the other way round.

WOHA, Iluma, Singapore, 2009
The pixelated exterior of Iluma, with six-sided crystals following the flowing forms and a spectrum of red-and-brown tessellated panels following the orthogonal.

'Trees', says Richard, 'don't experience a crisis of authenticity. They need a big enough planter, and in the tropics they grow happily up and down a building.' WOHA does not experience crises of authenticity, perhaps because it has moved on from the behaviours of a purely Western modernity and from its 20th-century echoes in Japanese modernity. And WOHA has moved on by revelling in its situation in the vast city-states of the emerging world (Shanghai, a city with a population the size of Australia's, has its own airline), and by deepening personal acceptances of actual histories in space – for Mun Summ the fact of living on a small urban island, for Richard the fact of growing up on the edge of a barely populated island continent with a very particular etiolated and

ancient landscape, and then of migrating into an Anglophone lobe of the Sinosphere, and the two of them immensely enjoying the 'new ugly' of a new aesthetic that comes from their open love of where they are.

WOHA, PARKROYAL on Pickering, Singapore, 2013
The rooms are lined with cabinetry, giving the impression of being in a timber box.

Companion to PARKROYAL on Pickering: Sauerbruch Hutton, Cologne Oval Offices, Cologne, Germany, 2010
Louisa Hutton uses colour to give an impression of natural origins.

Poolhouse 1, Home Counties, England[14]

Ushida Findlay, 2001

Kathryn Findlay was an exponent of and advocate for the conscious use of spatial intelligence in practice. Observing herself at work on two continents, she developed a full understanding of her mental space and used that to create and control a historically nuanced poetics. This case study traces the evolution of one design idea in her practice.

In the words of her obituary:

> Kathryn Findlay 26 Jan 1953 – 10 Jan 2014. The daughter of James, an Angus sheep farmer, and Elizabeth, Findlay was born in Finavon, Scotland. She studied at the Architectural Association in London in 1976, where she was taught by Peter Cook, founding member of the radical Archigram group, and Leon van Schaik, who inspired her interest in the idea of space as a solid matter that could be carved and sculpted.[15]

I have strong memories of Kathryn as a second-year student in my unit at the Architectural Association (AA). She took it upon herself to establish an enduring and often challenging friendship with me, one that survived my continental displacements and that flourished during my first decade in Australia, a period that coincided with her last decade in Japan; and after her return to the UK, and as practice professor at the University of Dundee, she invited me to give a lecture.[16] Kathryn had a more direct connection with me in Australia. In 1996 Barrie Kosky directed the Adelaide Festival, conceiving of it as a site at which 'dead art' is brought to life through performance. He asked me to programme the banks of the River Torrens with a series of architectural interventions that would bring the whole festival site alive for the event. Thinking of this terrain as laced with sites that epitomised aspects of the thinking that brought the city of Adelaide into being, I devised a curatorial framework using Robert Smithson's phrase 'Ruins of the Future' as its title.[17] Kathryn and her partner Eisaku who founded Ushida Findlay were among those invited to respond. In the booklet commemorating the festival, they wrote:

> The Siting: For two days we walked the banks of the River Torrens looking for the exact location of our installation, and we thought about what we had learned in our seven-day crash course in Australian culture. We then absorbed

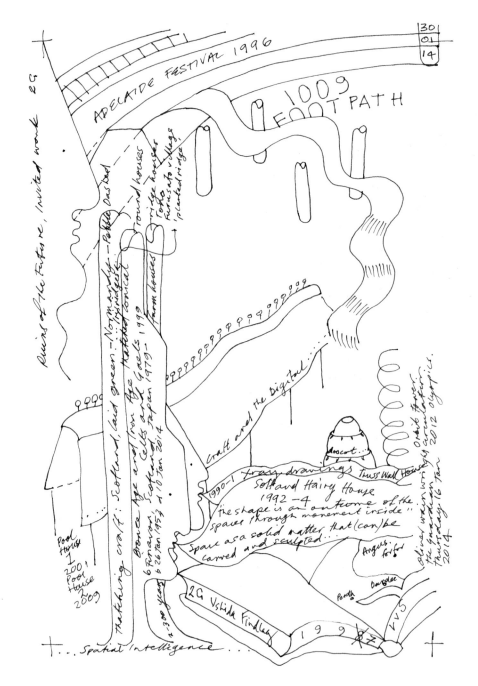

the space into our bodies in order to fix the place. The place we felt to be most accommodating only revealed itself in the last twenty minutes of our available time there. We sought 'points of tension' and points of 'take-off', some place where we could 'peel' the landscape from the surface of the ground to create a shelter with dialogue between the collective notion of shelter and the hosting geomorphology.[18]

Ushida Findlay, Poolhouse 1, Home Counties, England, 2001
Poolhouse 1 has a direct linkage to the ancient tradition in Japan and Europe of planting the thatched ridges of houses with irises, the roots of which bind the thatch together.

They peeled back the turf to reveal a map reference '1009 FOOTPATH' (the title they gave their installation), and in so doing suggested that the red earth of the Australian desert lay beneath the site. Then they floated a lyrical brushwood-thatched wave through the trees from the footpath to the bank of the river.

Last year, researching for this book, I suggested to Kathryn that one of my exemplars could be her thatched Poolhouse series (Poolhouse 1, 2001; Poolhouse 2, 2009). Convinced that Kathryn drew on deeply embedded poetic understandings of space and form, I was intrigued (in my re-reading) by the 'collective notion of shelter'. Our conversation was too late. Questioned, her architect daughter Miya Ushida observed that the thatching had been

Leon van Schaik, research ideogram, 30 January 2011
Drawn at the conclusion of researching the project.

Ushida Findlay, Poolhouse 2, Home Counties, England, 2009
Poolhouse 2 shows Ushida Findlay using thatch as a material that lends itself to the forms that emerge from algorithmic designing.

inspired by Japanese thatched farmhouses, many of which, two to three hundred years old, survive, and some of which, like Poolhouse 1, have planted ridges.

I was wondering whether Kathryn had seen the thatched ridges of Normandy, where traditionally the ridge is capped with clay planted with irises that bind the ridge through the roots extending from their rhizomes. Miya thought not. Then I searched for the Celtic and Gaelic history of thatched buildings and found an uncanny resemblance between traditional Celtic thatching in Scotland, in which the reeds are laid while green, and the green end fronds of the brush that Ushida Findlay (having noticed its use as fencing in the suburbs) used to construct their first thatch building, in Adelaide.[19] They also wrote (referring to the feel for 'the lie of the land' displayed by Colonel Light, founder of the city of Adelaide, as documented by Paul Carter, whose text on this framed the curatorial brief):

Ushida Findlay, *1009 FOOTPATH*, for 'Ruins of the Future', Adelaide Festival, Adelaide, 1996
(Above) This brush structure was the architects' first essay into thatch.
(Below) The map reference was located on the site and the turf 'peeled back' to reveal the legend '1009 FOOTPATH'.

We, Ushida Findlay, are outsiders and have come from Japan, not as a homogenous unit but as a hybrid mix of Japanese and Scottish cultural experience …

Coming from urban Japan, where the desire for certainty, closure and, above all, stability has smothered the existence of the mytho-poetical knowledge of the land, we empathise with Light's version. Perhaps in Australia the deep rift between the modern superego and the primal collective consciousness is most honestly addressed. It certainly was a welcome surprise to us to find it so. Australia has re-discovered that the mytho-poetic tells us of the nature within us all.[20]

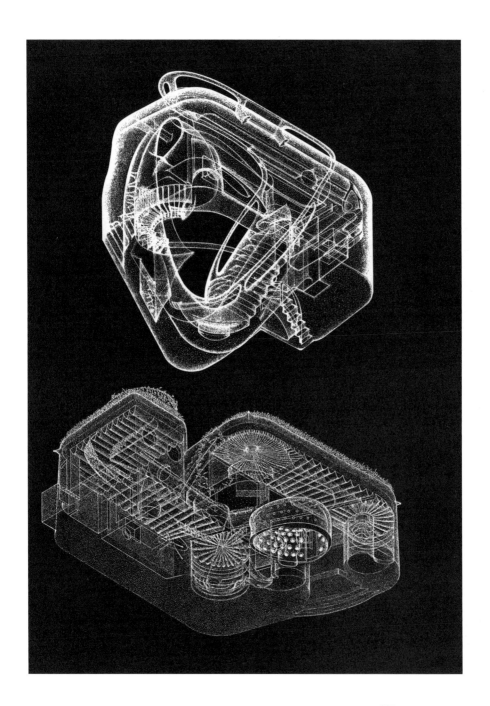

Planted roof ridges in
Shirakawa, Japan
Kathryn Findlay was
fascinated by these
traditional farmhouses.

There follows some agonising in the process of designing, which I characterized as follows:

> Ushida Findlay … acted out their obsession with the reinstatement of nature through building. [I had the Soft and Hairy House (1994) in mind.] A sweeping form bridged across a natural amphitheatre amidst imported trees. A brushwood feathering made a structure that denied the duality of horizontal and vertical and embraced the topological mathematics that is emerging as the latest geometry to be consumed by architects, although in their case 'explored' is the more appropriate term. This is a potent evocation of the post perspectival surface-space that computer aided reality is enabling.[21]

Ushida Findlay, Truss Wall
House, Tokyo, 1993, and
Soft and Hairy House,
Tokyo, 1994
'Slimy' drawings that Ushida
Findlay developed to reveal
the full spatiality of their
designs.

They concluded:

> We have come to realise that this is not about plugging something in, but finding a delicate point of interaction with the topography. This is pre-modern. … We have lost sight of the fact that land is a space-time matrix, where buildings have a far shorter life than the hosting topography. This

installation … address(es) the space-time matrix in which these Ruins of the Future reflect the shape of the city and the shape to which we must expect it, ultimately, to return.[22]

During the following two years, and at Kathryn's instigation, I crafted the 2G monograph on Ushida Findlay's Japanese work.[23] They concluded their Nexus statement by describing their exceptional drawing technique, something that Kathryn – knowing, I think, that if she could not draw her spatial intelligence or model it, she could not design with it – was already exploring in her second year at the AA:

> Through the pursuit of topologically-based designs, which matured in the
> Truss Wall House (1992-3) design, we have developed a new way of drawing.
> Through this we aspire to encapsulate the multi-dimensions of space as a
> transparent, viscous and continuous medium, simultaneously read as parts
> and whole… For us these drawings combine our concerns into a single
> plangent image, a frame that holds everything in view, and enables us to see
> what we do next.[24]

Companion to Poolhouse 1: Sarah Calburn, Sea House, Betty's Bay, South Africa, 2011
The landscape, as often in Calburn's architecture, is integral to the design.

References

1. Leon van Schaik, *Mastering Architecture: Becoming a Creative Innovator in Practice*, Wiley (Chichester), 2005: see discussion of Gardner's concept of 'mastery' on p 14, and of Collins's concept of tri-polarity on pp 106 and 234.
2. See Martyn Hook, *The Act of Reflective Practice: The Emergence of Iredale Pedersen Hook Architects*, unpublished PhD thesis, RMIT, Melbourne, 2008.
3. They met at Queensland Institute of Technology, now Queensland University of Technology.
4. See Leon van Schaik, 'Differentiation in Vital Practice: An Analysis Using RMIT University of Technology and Design Interfaces with Architects', in Pia Ednie-Brown, Mark Burry and Andrew Burrow (eds), *The Innovative Imperative: Architectures of Vitality*, Architectural Design (AD) series (Wiley, London), January/February (no 1), 2013, pp 106–13.
5. See Michael Christensen, *The Practice of m3architecture: The Managerial Frame Work*, unpublished Master's thesis, RMIT, Melbourne, 2010; Michael Banney, *The Practice of m3architecture: The Intellectual Frame Work*, unpublished Master's thesis, RMIT, Melbourne, 2010; Michael Lavery, *The Practice of m3architecture: The Social Context*, unpublished Master's thesis, RMIT, Melbourne, 2010; and Benjamin Vielle, *The Practice of m3architecture: The Relationship between Architecture and Art Practice*, unpublished Master's thesis, RMIT, Melbourne, 2010.
6. See Gaston Bachelard, *The Poetics of Reverie* [*La Poétique de la rêverie*, 1960], translated by Daniel Russell, Beacon Press (Boston, MA), 1971.
7. Robin Dunbar, 'The Bright Stuff: Only the Smartest Creatures Have What It Takes to Make Friends, Says Evolutionary Psychologist Robin Dunbar, University of

Oxford', *New Scientist*, 24 May 2014, p 42.

8. See Nikos Papastergiadis, *Cosmopolitanism and Culture*, Polity Press (London), 2012.

9. Cao Xueqin, *The Story of the Stone* [mid-18th century, also known as *The Dream of the Red Chamber*], *Vol 1: The Golden Days*, translated by David Hawkes, Penguin (London), 1973.

10. See Leon van Schaik, 'Between Abstraction and Cultural Reference: House at Morley Road', *Singapore Architect Journal*, no 201, 1999, pp 24–31.

11. This text is adapted from a review in *Architecture Australia*, September/October 2013, pp 24–33.

12. Edward St Aubyn, *Lost for Words*, Picador (London), 2014, p 240.

13. St Aubyn 2014, p 235.

14 A version of this text was published as an obituary on the Architecture Australia website on 5 February 2014.

15. Oliver Wainwright, obituary in the *Guardian*, 15 January 2014.

16. Leon van Schaik, 'Energising Cities', in the Energising Cities Lecture Series, University of Dundee, Scotland, 1 November 2006.

17. Robert Smithson, 'A Tour of the Monuments of Passaic, New Jersey' [1967], in Nancy Holt (ed), *The Writings of Robert Smithson*, New York University Press (New York), 1979.

18. Leon van Schaik (ed), *Ruins of the Future*, RMIT (Melbourne), November 2000, p 17.

19. Leon van Schaik (ed), *Ushida Findlay* (2G, no 6), Editorial Gustavo Gili (Barcelona), 1997, p 88.

20. Ushida Findlay in Schaik (ed) 2000, p 16.

21. Schaik (ed) 2000, p 8.

22. *Ibid*, p 17.

23. Schaik (ed) 1997. This included a section on the Adelaide Festival project, pp 86–91.

24. *Ibid*, p 135.

Conclusion

A Reflection on Practical Poetics

For architects, poetics is a sensibility arising from their accumulated experience of place and space, experience that is mediated by their learned expectations – the values imbued through interaction with mentors, peers, challengers and fellow citizens. Poetics suffuses the mental space of designers, the constellation of attitudes, skills, approaches, modes and manners that form the platform on which their designing occurs.

This book focuses on a particular strand in current practice, a strand that seeks to ameliorate the world as we find it. There are no large-scale, stand-alone projects here. These are not grandiose projects marshalled in support of dictatorial regimes or global sporting empires, and corporate branding is ignored. The jostling towers, retail fit-outs and stadia that catch media attention are all symptoms of the pathology of the times. They are created outside any possible poetics discourse, glossy shiny objects that float around the world detached from the architectural reality of particular places. Future generations will look back on this architecture of conspicuous consumption and marvel at just how blind these practices were to the situation to which they give expression so unconsciously today

What this book concerns itself with are projects and practices working on the adaptive change that cities need to make as they deal with the shifting conditions of our times. They are modest, local and grounded. They speak of a practice that is about wellbeing at home, about physical and mental recreation, about being civil and civic and about changing ways of relating to natural forces. These are the architectural practices that are becoming more and more important as we move into the Anthropocene.

How does poetics play out when such ameliorating architects design? How are ideas formed in contemporary, modest and consciously appropriate design? The practices whose projects are in this book are smaller, ideas-driven practices. Their scale enables them to construct shared and shareable mental spaces. These spaces are created through conversations between principals that are then structured into the practices through narratives woven around the portfolios of works and through shared anecdotes. Conversation suffuses the case studies.[1] The mental spaces of each practice are reinforced in the ways studios are arranged, collaborations structured.[2] And this book seeks out in each case to study a threshold at which a poetic mental frame is established and designing cascades forward.

Architecture is a practice based on a body of knowledge, and as a profession it has a duty to apply that knowledge in the best interests of society.[3] Architecture that serves only the elites as they aggrandise themselves, in short-term denial of climate change and in denial of the damage in store for the body politic as the gap between rich and middle to poor widens, betrays this trust. The knowledge base of such architecture is self-referential, self-contained and almost purely decorative in intent. Its protagonists are shamelessly autocratic. This book does not concern itself with this aberrant architecture. It has relevance for a different kind of practice now emerging. My book *Spatial Intelligence: New Futures for Architecture* identifies a new role for architectural intelligence, and by implication suggests a new realm for poetics that deploys spatial thinking in the reconfiguration of the use of cities in the information age.[4] This argument has been hailed by Dan Hill, an executive at the think tank Future Cities Catapult.[5] It is also partly explored in AD *Pavilions, Pop-Ups and Parasols*, an issue of AD which argues that a new architectural form is emerging around the world.[6] In public places a progressive architecture is being commissioned to promote open-ended, undetermined, lightly programmed or un-programmed interactions between people. This could be another book …

This book however concerns the architecture that matters as communities seek to ameliorate the current pathologies of economic and social inequity.

The architects here discussed have a knowledge base grounded in the spatial intelligence of everyone. These practices have researched their histories in space and have consciously honed their spatial thinking. They serve the middle ground and drive hard to use their architectural intelligence to help more people. This architecture is modest in scale, grounded in particular geographical and cultural places. It is vital to communities in their quests for making home, feeding body, mind and soul, healing their urban environment and capturing a sense of nature in ever larger cities.

Architects choose between these three spheres of practice – designing for corporates, ameliorating cities or envisaging new roles for architects in the information age – and as professionals they are responsible for their choice, so it should be made consciously. I hope this book helps articulate what one of those choices entails: these are, without exception, practices happily engaged in meaningful change.

References

1. See Gordon Pask, *Conversation, Cognition and Learning: A Cybernetic Theory and Methodology*, Elsevier (Amsterdam, Oxford and London), 1975.
2. See Ramon Prat, Anna Tetas and Carles Poy (eds), *Barcelona Lab*, Actar (Barcelona), 2003.
3. See Leon van Schaik, *Mastering Architecture:*

Becoming a Creative Innovator in Practice, Wiley (Chichester), 2005, p 14.
4. Leon van Schaik, *Spatial Intelligence: New Futures for Architecture*, Wiley (Chichester), 2008.
5. Dan Hill, 'Urban Parasites, Data-Driven Urbanism, and the Case for Architecture', in Alastair Townsend (ed), *A+U:*

Data-Driven Cities, November 2014, pp 6–10.
6. Leon van Schaik and Fleur Watson (eds), *Pavilions, Pop-Ups and Parasols: The Impact of Real and Virtual Meeting on Physical Space*, Architectural Design (AD) series (Wiley, London), May/June (no 3), 2015.

Select Bibliography

Bachelard, Gaston, *The Poetics of Space* [*La Poétique de l'espace*, 1957], translated by Maria Jolas, Beacon Press (Boston, MA), 1969 (first published in English in 1964 with the subtitle: *The Classic Look at How We Experience Intimate Places*)

Beilharz, Peter, *Postmodern Socialism: Romanticism, City and State*, Melbourne University Press (Melbourne), 1994

Blythe, Richard and Leon van Schaik, 'What If Design Practice Matters?', in Murray Fraser (ed), *Design Research in Architecture*, Ashgate (London), 2013, pp 53–70

Brown, Mark Burry and Andrew Burrow (eds), *The Innovation Imperative: Architectures of Vitality*, Architectural Design (AD) series (Wiley, London), January/February (no 1), 2013, pp 106–13

Cao Xueqin, *The Story of the Stone* [mid-18th century, also known as *The Dream of the Red Chamber*], *Vol 1: The Golden Days*, translated by David Hawkes, Penguin (London), 1973

Collins, Randall, *The Sociology of Philosophies: A Global Theory of Intellectual Change*, Harvard University Press (Cambridge, MA), 2000

Dawkins, Richard, *The Selfish Gene* [1976, revised 2006], Folio Society (London), 2011

Debord, Guy, *The Society of the Spectacle* [*La Société du spectacle*, 1967], translated by Fredy Perlman et al, Black & Red (Detroit), 1983

Evans, Robin, *Translations from Drawing to Building*, Architectural Association (London), 1997

Fisher, Philip, *Wonder, The Rainbow, and the Aesthetics of Rare Experiences*, Harvard University Press (Cambridge, MA), 1998

Fletcher, Banister, *A History of Architecture on the Comparative Method* [1896], Athlone Press (London), 1963

Frampton, Kenneth, *Studies in Tectonic Culture*, The MIT Press (Cambridge, MA and London), 1995

Frayn, Michael, *The Human Touch*, Picador (New York), 2006

Geertz, Clifford, *The Interpretation of Culture*, Basic Books (New York), 1973

Goffman, Erving, *Asylums*, Pelican (London), 1961

Grotowski, Jerzy and Eugenio Barba, *Towards a Poor Theatre*, Methuen Drama (London), 1994

Kahneman, Daniel, *Thinking, Fast and Slow*, Allen Lane (London), 2011

Lanza, Robert and Bob Berman, *Biocentrism: How Life and Consciousness are the Keys to Understanding the True Nature of the Universe*, Ben Bella Books (Dallas, TX), 2009

Lethaby, WR, *Architecture, Nature and Magic* [1928; revised version of *Architecture, Mysticism and Myth*, 1892], Gerald Chatsworth & Co (London), 1956

Li Shiqiao, *Understanding the Chinese City*, Sage (London), 2014

Lim, William SW, *Asian Alterity: With Special Reference to Architecture and Urbanism Through the Lens of Cultural Studies*, World Scientific Publishing (Singapore), 2007

MacFarlane, Robert, *The Wild Places*, Granta Publications (London), 2008

Malafouris, Lambros, *How Things Shape the Mind: A Theory of Material Engagement*, The MIT Press (Cambridge, MA), 2013

Mallgrave, Harry Francis, *Gottfried Semper: Architect of the Nineteenth Century*, Yale University Press (New Haven, CT and London), 1996

Manguel, Alberto, *The Library at Night*, Yale University Press (New Haven, CT), 2008

McLuhan, Marshall, *The Gutenberg Galaxy*, Routledge & Kegan Paul (London), 1967

Norberg-Schulz, Christian, *Intentions in Architecture*, The MIT Press (Cambridge, MA), 1963

Pallasmaa, Juhani, *The Eyes of the Skin: Architecture and the Senses*, Wiley (Chichester), 2005

Papastergiadis, Nikos, *Cosmopolitanism and Culture*, Polity Press (London), 2012

Pask, Gordon, *Conversation, Cognition and Learning: A Cybernetic Theory and Methodology*, Elsevier (Amsterdam, Oxford and London), 1975

Piketty, Thomas, *Capital in the Twenty-First Century*, Harvard University Press (Cambridge, MA), 2013

Popper, Karl R, *The Logic of Scientific Discovery* [1959], Hutchinson (London), 1980

Prat, Ramon, Anna Tetas and Carles Poy (eds), *Barcelona Lab*, Actar (Barcelona), 2003

Rasmussen, Steen Eiler, *Experiencing Architecture* [1959], The MIT Press (Cambridge, MA), 1964

Richards IA, *Practical Criticism A Study of Literary Judgment* [1929], Harcourt Brace World (New York), 1956

Rossi, Aldo, *The Architecture of the City* [*L'architettura della città*, 1966], translated by Diane Ghirardo and Joan Ockman, The MIT Press (Cambridge, MA and London), 1982

Rossi, Aldo, *A Scientific Autobiography* [*Autobiografia scientifica*, 1981], translated by Lawrence Venuti, The MIT Press (Cambridge, MA and London), 1982

Rowe, Colin, *The Architecture of Good Intentions*, Academy Editions (London), 1994

Rowe, Colin, *The Mathematics of the Ideal Villa and Other Essays*, The MIT Press (Cambridge, MA and London), 1976

Rowe, Colin and Fred Koetter, *Collage City*, The MIT Press (Cambridge, MA and London), 1978

Ruscha, Ed, *Every Building on the Sunset Strip*, Ed Ruscha (Los Angeles) 1966

Rykwert, Joseph, *On Adam's House in Paradise: The Idea of the Primitive Hut in Architectural History*, Museum of Modern Art (New York), 1972

Schaik, Leon van, 'Architectural Reality: A Continuum Concept', in Mary Wall (ed), *AA Files*, no 28, Architectural Association (London), 1994, pp 12–15

Schaik, Leon van, *Mastering Architecture: Becoming a Creative Innovator in Practice*, Wiley (Chichester), 2005

Schaik, Leon van, *Poetics in Architecture*, Wiley (Chichester), 2002

Schaik, Leon van, *Spatial Intelligence: New Futures for Architecture*, Wiley (Chichester), 2008

Schaik, Leon van and Geoffrey London (with an essay by Beth George), *Procuring Innovative Architecture*, Routledge (London), 2010

Schaik, Leon van, 'Differentiation in Vital Practice: An Analysis using RMIT University of Technology and Design Interfaces with Architects', in Pia Ednie-

Schaik, Leon van, with Tom Holbrook and Deborah Saunt , 'RMIT Practice Research Program: The Practice Makes Perfect', *Architectural Review*, vol 234, no 1,400, October 2013, pp 82–8

Schaik, Leon van and Anna Johnson, *Architecture & Design, By Practice, By Invitation: Design Practice Research at RMIT*, onepointsixone (Melbourne), 2011

Schumacher, Thomas L, *The Danteum*, Princeton Architectural Press (New York), 1985

Scott Brown, Denise and Robert Venturi, *Learning from Las Vegas*, The MIT Press (Cambridge, MA), 1972

Stamm, Marcelo, *Constellating Creativity*, Lyon Housemuseum (Melbourne), 2014

Starr, S Frederick, *Melnikov: Solo Architect in a Mass Society*, Princeton University Press (Princeton, NJ), 1981

Turner, Mark, *The Origin of Ideas: Blending, Creativity, and the Human Spark*, Oxford University Press (Oxford), 2014

Turnovsky, Jan, *The Poetics of a Wall Projection* [*Die Poetik eines Mauervorsprungs*, 1985], translated by Kent Kleinman, AA Publications (London), 2009

Vesely, Dalibor, 'Architecture and the Conflict of Representation', in Mary Wall (ed), *AA Files*, no 8, Architectural Association (London), 1985, pp 21–38

Vesely, Dalibor, *Architecture in the Age of Divided Representation: The Question of Creativity in the Shadow of Production*, The MIT Press (Cambridge, MA), 2004

Watkins, Alfred, *The Old Straight Track*, Abacus (London), 1974

West, Geoffrey, 'The Surprising Math of Cities and Corporations', TED Talk, July, 2011, www.ted.com/talks/geoffrey_west_the_surprising_math_of_cities_and_corporations

Wijdeveld, Paul, *Ludwig Wittgenstein, Architect*, The MIT Press (Cambridge, MA), 1994

Wilson, Vicky and Tom Neville (eds), *Sensing Spaces: Architecture Reimagined*, exhibition catalogue, Royal Academy of Arts (London), 2014

Index

Figures in *italic* type refer to illustrations.

Picture Credits

The author and the publisher gratefully acknowledge the people who gave their permission to reproduce material in the book. While every effort has been made to contact copyright holders for their permission to reprint material the publishers would be grateful to hear from any copyright holder who is not acknowledged here and will undertake to rectify any errors or omissions in future editions.

Front cover image © Peter Bennetts/KGA

p 8 © Peter Lyssiotis; p 10 Photograph: James Harris/Royal Academy of Arts, © Grafton Architects; p 11 (l) Photograph: James Harris/Royal Academy of Arts, © Pezo von Ellrichshausen
p 11 (r) © Li Xiaodong; pp 14, 32, 35, 36, 37, 40, 42, 50, 57 (b), 58, 60, 62, 66, 78, 81, 88, 91 (b), 92, 93 (t), 94, 102, 108, 116, 118, 121 (b), 122, 124, 129, 130, 138, 146, 156, 164, 172, 180, 194, 202, 210, 218, 226, 229 (t & b) © Leon van Schaik; p 15 From Il Danteum di Terragni, originally published in by Italian Officinai Edizioni, Rome 1980; p 16 From Il Danteum di Terragni, originally published in by Italian Officinai Edizioni, Rome 1980; p 17 © Getty Images/ Alan Copson; p 19 Artist: Thomas Rowlandson. Oxford, Science Archive, © 2014. Photo Art Media/ Heritage Images/Scala, Florence; p 20 © MVRDR, photographer Rob 't Hart; p 22 (t) Rossi, Aldo (1931-1997) and Braghieri, Gianni (b. 1945), © 2014. Digital image, The Museum of Modern Art, New York/Scala, Florence; p 22 (b) © Pkemp | Dreamstime.com; p 23 © Juergen Schonnop | Dreamstime.com; p 24 © Milosk50 | Dreamstime.com; p 25 © Geoffrey Allerton | Dreamstime.com; p 26 © Ihsan Gercelman | Dreamstime.com; p 27 © Soman; pp 34, 38 © Richard Blythe; p 39 Joey Verge /Creative Commons Attribution Wikipedia; p 40 © Leon van Schaik; p 42 © Leon van Schaik; pp 43, 44 (t), 46, 47 © Alex de Rijke/dRMM Architects; pp 44 (b), 45, 48 © dRMM Architects; p 49 © Flores & Prats, Photographer Eugeni Pons; pp 52 (t & b), 57 (t) © John Brown/Housebrand; pp 53, 54, 55 © Housebrand; pp 30, 59, 61, 63, 64 © Julian Feary/Feary+Heron Architects; p 65 © Martin Charles / RIBA Library Photographs Collection; p 68 © The Estate of Howard Arkley, Licensed by Kalli Rolfe Contemporary Art; p 69 © Jan van Schaik/MvS Architects; p 70 © MvS Architects; pp 71, 72 © Peter Bennetts/Minifie van Schaik Architects; p 73 © Alice Clancy/TAKA; p 76 © Sean Godsell Architects in Association with Peddle Thorp Architects/Earl Carter; pp 82, 85 © By Joost; pp 83, 84, 85 (t) © By Joost/Earl Carter; p 86 © CJ Lim; pp 89, 90, 91 (t) © Jo Van Den Berghe; p 93 (b) © Alice Clancy/Clancy Moore; pp 95, 97 (t), 98, 99 © Peter Hogg + Toby Reed Architects, photo John Gollings; pp 96, 97 (b) © Peter Hogg + Toby Reed Architects; p 100 Scanned From Melnikov: Solo Architect in a Mass Society, originally published Princeton University Press 1981; pp 101, 103 (t), 104 (b) © Peter Hogg + Toby Reed Architects, photography Sam Reed; pp 102, 104 (t) © Peter Hogg & Toby Reed Architects; p 105 © AL_A; pp 107, 109, 110, 111, 112, 113 © Kurtogpi Architects/Sigurgeir Sigurjónsson; p 114 © McGarry Ní Éanaigh Architects, photographer Richard Hatch; p 117 © Sean Godsell Architects, photographer Earl Carter; pp 119, 120, 121 (t) © Sean Godsell Architects in association with Peddle Thorpe Architects; p 123 (t) © Archive Leitner/Vienna; p 123 (b) Jan Manu/Creative Commons Attribution Wikipedia; pp 126, 131, 132 © Peter Bennetts/Crab Studio; pp 127, 128 © Crab Studio; p 133 Cassandra Fahey/Creative Commons Attribution Wikipedia; pp 136, 147, 148, 154 © Tim Crocker; p 140 © Kerstin Thompson Architects; pp 142, 143, 144 © Kerstin Thompson Architects/Trevor Mein; p 145 © Trevor Mein/meinphoto; p 149 © Louis Hellman/ CZWG Architects LLP; pp 150, 152, 153 © CZWG Architects LLP; p 155 © Martine De Maeseneer Architects, photographer Filip Dujardin; pp 158, 159, 160, 163 (t), 182, 183, 184 © O'Donnell + Tuomey Architects; pp 161, 162, 165, 166 (t & b) © Dennis Gilbert / VIEW; p 163 (b) © Photography John Gollings/SXWA; p 167 (t & b), 168, 169, 170 © DSDHA Ltd; pp 171, 186 © Lyons/John Gollings; p 173 © Pipop Boosarakumwadi | Dreamstime. com; p 174 © Pod666 | Dreamstime.com; pp 176, 177, 178, 179 Courtesy Hargreaves/University of Cincinnati; p 181 © Zoa3d Budapest/Central European University; p 187 © SLV/The Rose Series P. 2653; p 188 (t) © NLA/ Sievers, Wolfgang/Bates, Smart and McCutcheon; p 188 (b) © RMIT University Archives; pp 189, 190 (t) © Lyons Architecture with NMBW Architecture Studio, Minifie van Schaik Architects, Harrison and White Architects, Maddison Architects; p 190 (b) © Photograph Paolo Tonato/Grafton Architects; p 192 © Peter Bennetts; pp 195, 196, 197, 200 © Jon Linkins/m3architecture; p 198 © Brian Hooper/m3architecture in association with Brian Hooper Architect; p 199 © m3architecture;
p 201 Cjc13/Creative Commons Attribution Wikipedia; pp 204, 207 (t & b), 208 (t) © Edward Hendricks/W Architects Pte Ltd; p 206 (t & b) W Architects Pte Ltd; p 208 (b) © Stefano Boeri Architetti; pp 209, 211, 213, 214, 215 © Peter Bennetts/KGA; p 212 © Kristin Green Architecture; pp 216, 232 © Sarah Calburn Architects; pp 219, 220, 221, 222, 223, 224 (t) © Patrick Bingham Hall/WOHA; p 224 (b) © Thvietz/Dreamstime.com; p 227 © David Churchill; p 228 © Photo Katsuhisa Kida/Ushida Findlay; p 230 © Kathryn Findlay/Ushida Findlay; p 231 © Takeshi Nishio | Dreamstime.com.